RELIGIONLESS CHRISTIANITY

RELIGIONLESS CHRISTIANITY

Dietrich Bonhoeffer in Troubled Times

JEFFREY C. PUGH

t & t clark

Published by T&T Clark International
A Continuum Imprint
The Tower Building, 11 York Road, London SE1 7NX
80 Maiden Lane, Suite 704, New York, NY 10038

www.continuumbooks.com

British Library Cataloguing-in-Publication Data
A catalogue record for this book is available from the British Library.

ISBN-10: HB: 0-567-03258-2
         PB: 0-567-03259-0
ISBN-13: HB: 978-0-567-03258-4
         PB: 978-0-567-03259-1

Typeset by Newgen Imaging Systems Pvt Ltd, Chennai, India
Printed and bound in Great Britain by MPG Books Ltd, Bodmin, Cornwall

To Jan Rivero, companion in life
and
love of students

CONTENTS

FOREWORD

You can walk along any street or mingle in any reasonable crowd and ask to see if anyone can identify Dietrich Bonhoeffer. Unless you are on a campus or at a church convention, no one will step up to try. Even where his name makes its way dimly into someone's consciousness, you are not likely to get any takers who have precise answers, unless you have stumbled into divinity school wings of universities or religious studies classrooms in some colleges which offer ample curricular choices. There someone might know who you are talking about, but don't ask her to pronounce B-o-n-h-o-e-f-f-e-r satisfactorily in the ears of a German speaker. It cannot be said that Western culture is so familiar with his name, or that of any twentieth century theologian, that we can rightfully complain that there's been too much attention to this candidate for theological celebrity status. Yet most people who comment in essays or at book-length on the man and his thought feel they have to apologize for Bonhoeffer and explain themselves to us. Jeffrey Pugh is aware of the dangers of over-familiarity, explains his interest, and then happily moves on with dispatch.

For contrasts, mention Bonhoeffer among religious scholars and specialists in theology, and the opposite case presents itself. 'Oh, Bonhoeffer? We've moved on. Who reads him anymore, or who should? We have passed through four or five stages of post-this or post-that and certainly post-Bonhoeffer theory. He and the other theological B's – Barth, Brunner, Baillie, Bultmann, Berdyaev, Buber and the rest are so *modern* and we are post-modern. He's only interesting to people who belong to a Bonhoeffer cult. Move on with us. *Yawn.*' So commentators on his thought – and their numbers have not even begun to dwindle – also have to apologize for him to them and explain their interest to us. Professor Pugh does a bit of that explaining, but almost at once he engages us with stories of the life and themes of this young theologian who was executed in Germany one month before the European phase of World War II ended.

I apologize if my first paragraph sounded a bit snobbish about the people who don't preoccupy themselves with theology and theologians, and a bit jaded about those who worry about 'who's in' and 'who's out'. I have always thought that the best responses one can provide and the best service one can perform when dealing with anyone who was significant in the past is to plunge in, acquaint readers with the person and the issues, and move on. Pugh certainly does that, and he makes the case. As for the writings, one has to say that the canon of Bonhoefferiana is not yet closed; new documents keep turning up, and fresh comment concerning his whole corpus keeps appearing. As for the question of a Bonhoeffer cult, let me agree that the temptation to make an icon of him is strong, especially in a time when there is a dearth of heroes. And as for his currency and promise, let me simply ask veterans and newcomers alike to read on. There seem, to me at least, to be any number of unresolved and irresolvable but important issues that come up and will continue to come up with Bonhoeffer studies.

Will it change the world if a new generation succeeds in resolving some of the issues, making sense of some of the paradoxes, and finding paths outlined by Bonhoeffer? Let's try an analogy, hyperbolic as it may seem to be. William Carlos Williams wrote:

It is difficult
To get the news from poems
Yet men die miserably every day
For lack
Of what is found there –

It is difficult to get 'news' of 'meaning of life' questions or answers from many theologians, but when they take up the right issues and deal with them passionately but are ignored, people may not die miserably but they will not live the enriched lives for which they were destined, according to their belief in being made 'in the image of God'. Cheery greeting cards, 'Have a nice day!' partings, best-selling self-help books, Prosperity Gospel pitches, will not do when life and death issues are at stake. Bonhoeffer was living 'life and death issues' for his last dozen years, and he wrote eloquently about how he dealt with them. Jeffrey Pugh takes seriously his personal engagements, with all their paradoxes and complexity, helps sort them out, and deliberates about their meanings for today.

Authors of Forewords know the rules of the game: comment on the credibility of the author being forwarded, something which is easy to do in Pugh's case; assure readers that the topic is rich in promise and the treatment is rewarding; don't reveal details of the plot – and get out of the way.

One of my favorite contentions about and tests for books, borrowed from Eugen Rosenstock-Huessy, is this: 'One book is about one thing, at least the good ones are.' They can be long and complex, like *War and Peace* or *The Decline and Fall of the Roman Empire* or short and complex, like *Winnie the Pooh,* but if the author has not located and focused on 'one thing', she is not likely to be helpful or to make an enduring impact on readers.

Pugh's 'one thing' among the Bonhoeffer themes is the concept of 'religionless Christianity', as envisioned sketchily in letters the condemned theologian wrote from prison. No, the concept is not oxymoronic, but it does demand careful unpacking. Bonhoeffer pictured a 'world come of age', in which people are to serve Jesus Christ without the trappings of religion, and even, in some ways, to act as if God did not exist. Yet Pugh shows that such a description, and the beginnings of prescriptions which accompanied it, did not leave Bonhoeffer in atheism, at least not in any run-of-the-mill or non-Christian ways. It did not distract him from his task of writing a Christ-centred *Ethics.* While many academic writers do their analysing and expounding and then drop the subject to go their way, Pugh also has an interest in how 'religionless Christianity' works itself out in the believing community and how it works among those not involved with church or Christianity.

He does not set out to legitimate Bonhoeffer by saying how relevant he is to our very changed situation, but so obvious are some hints and connections that Pugh does not resist the temptation to comment, and I am happy for that. He is not an ideologue or a screecher, but it is clear that his conscience won't let him pass by when contemporary outrages are all too apparent. He never over-presses the point, and more frequently than not turns what would be comments into questions which a conscientious reader will feel called to address in his or her own contexts.

He wrestles with large questions. Was Bonhoeffer's vision accurate? It certainly seems to be so in many sectors of Europe, where church participation dwindles and secularization by every definition grows ever more visible and potent. Yet, around the world there seems to be as much as ever of religion, Christianity, myth, symbol, ritual and at least 'pop-metaphysics', Christian explanations of and belief in the meaning of it all. Was he faithful to the Christ he set out to serve in the larger culture? Bonhoeffer died before he could detail his own vision of outcomes, but Pugh can rely on more than six decades of discussion, and brings tentative and provocative conclusions to the attention of readers.

No book is going to resolve all the contradictions, move beyond the paradoxes or solve all the puzzles from those late prison writings.

Jeffrey Pugh, however, makes substantial gains and offers contributions for those who would understand, and gives us tools and means for carrying the interpretive and critical tasks further.

Martin E. Marty
Emeritus
The University of Chicago

PREFACE

We live in troubled times. This may seem like a disingenuous statement. Which age has not lived in troubled times? It would appear that
trouble is the default position for life on the planet earth. But there
are some elements of this particular age that point to its own set of
unique circumstances. For one, we have amassed the self-destructive
power with our weaponry that potentially does hold us all hostages to
the fears we have created of world-wide destruction. No less real, but
more subtle, is our eroding environment and the catastrophic consequences of pursuing present courses of living that would endanger the
planet itself.

In the midst of these concerns, we are presently engaged in one
of humankind's perpetual struggles, this time framed by the political
order as the 'war on terror', though if were not this conflict it would be
another. Some see this as the challenge of our times and they have
responded by creating more war and more terror for future generations by policies that all but ensure that conflict will be an ever-present
reality. This conflict is complicated and the historical roots are inter-
twined with interests that are global in scope. If the threads of this are
unraveled they would reveal a nexus of actors in the arms, energy and
political world that have vested interests in not seeking resolution with
those who are currently arrayed against the West. When Augustine said
in *The City of God* that the state is like a large-scale crime syndicate he
could not have imagined how powerful those words would resonate
with our own times.

The global nature of this struggle is real and the damage inflicted
upon the innocent is widespread. Christians in whatever their social
location are being challenged with claims upon their lives and loyalties
that will only grow more intense as this struggle escalates in the near
future. I write from within American society and I must confess to a
sense of dis-ease about what happens here if another terrorist attack
takes place within the boundaries of this country. There are opportun-
ists who will take this as the occasion to fundamentally change our
society, and not for the better. We are not alone in this regard.

There are already forces present in many areas that would seek to
remake the world in the image of what they believe to be the best possible of all worlds. They take actions that pull the rest of the world into
their orbit and do so at the highest levels of government. What is the
Christian who is committed to following Christ supposed to do in these

circumstances? How do we find the ability to discern where something dark and evil, justifying itself as necessary for survival, is at work in the structures of society? How do we bear the grace of reconciliation to a world in love with its own self-destruction?

There are a multitude of voices that have their own answers to these questions, not all of them friendly to faith. This book has been written because I believe that in Dietrich Bonhoeffer's struggle with the destruction of his age we may find wisdom and perspective for our time. We look at his life and come away with different thoughts and perspectives on it because he was so conflicted himself. The Bonhoeffer of *Discipleship* and Finkenwalde is not the same Bonhoeffer who works in the *Abwehr* and conspires to rid the world of Hitler. There are continuities of thought throughout his life, but historical circumstances changed him, as they do all of us.

Bonhoeffer continues to exercise our imaginations because he was an ordinary man caught in extraordinary times. He was a brilliant theologian and a sensitive soul, but it was the challenges of his times and his response to them that call forth our admiration and curiosity. Oddly enough there are people today whose first thought is what would Bonhoeffer do? And the truth is we don't know, because Bonhoeffer never believed in absolute rules. He responded as a Christian rooted in the realities of the moment. And those concrete moments coloured his actions in ways that seem quite contradictory to us looking at them from the position of today.

One reality that remained constant throughout his life, though, is found in his writings from beginning to end. This is the question of what shape does Christ take in the world? How does Christ and the community founded in his name make itself manifest in the midst of struggles and conflicts? This was his true north star in his life and his theology. It also meant great anguish on his part when the church failed so miserably in its encounter with the Nazi regime.

So, it is with that perspective that I struggled my way through the book in your hands. In working my way through this I start with the different ways Bonhoeffer has been appropriated in the contemporary context and move to a short treatment of his life. From there, I explore the dimensions of how the 'world come of age' that Bonhoeffer probed in his prison captivity has become manifest in the present day. I then explore the role of religion and its power in the contemporary world to fuel those engaged in the conflicts of our age. Finally, I deal with whether the church does become visible in the midst of all the forces that call for our allegiances in the contemporary age. If it is to become a visible sign of God's desire for human life it may have to take leave of the Christian religion.

This can be a startling word, but in some ways it was what Bonhoeffer was trying to express with the term 'religionless Christianity'. Is such a thing possible? Can there be Christianity without religion? Would this type of Christianity be any more faithful to the Gospel of Jesus Christ than the one that surrendered to, even welcomed, Hitler? It may certainly be the case that faithfulness in our present age is an impossible task, but with God all things are possible.

If the church is to offer a word in these particular troubled times, it may have to be one that is radically different than what we presently experience. This word will undoubtedly come from those who know the reality of suffering and know its power to shape us for good or ill. In this way, I would like to suggest that Bonhoeffer's prison writings are particularly poignant places to reflect upon when thinking about our response to the present forces that seek dominance in the world. Many who rely on their own power will not find a comfortable or useful word in Bonhoeffer's appeal to powerlessness, but for those who understand what Bonhoeffer was struggling with, they may find in him needed wisdom for the church today.

With this book, I have become aware as never before of the provisionary nature of writing. There is so much left to say, but I had only so many words. In the end, I just had to let go and hope for another chance to express my thoughts. I also became aware of how deep my indebtedness is to those who in their own way inspire me to write. I am deeply appreciative of Thomas Kraft and those at T & T Clark/ Continuum for their willingness to publish yet another book on Dietrich Bonhoeffer. I have benefited deeply over the years from my teachers and colleagues. I am deeply grateful to John Godsey and Larry Rasmussen, teachers and mentors at Wesley Seminary in Washington, DC who first alerted me to the fact that there was someone here worth a second look. From there the list only grows. I am especially appreciative of my colleagues in the International Bonhoeffer Society and beyond who have been my companions and teachers for many years. Persons such as Lori Brandt Hale, John Matthews, Nancy Farrell, Jean Bethke Elshtain, Wayne Floyd, Geffrey Kelly, Mark Randall, John de Gruchy, Victoria Barnett, Lisa Dahill, Mark Blocker, Clifford Green, Fritz de Lange, Alice Bond, Peter Frick, Martin Rumscheidt, Stanley Hauerwas, and Charles Marsh have enriched my life in ways they may not be aware of, though several of them may disagree strongly with what I have argued here. I am also deeply grateful to Martin Marty for his gracious Forward to this text.

I am appreciative of my colleagues at Elon University who have made Elon such a wonderful place to fulfil my vocation. Special thanks to John Sullivan, Rebecca Todd Peters and Tripp York for reading this manuscript and asking questions and offering suggestions that have only made this a better text. I am also thankful for my colleagues in the department of Religious Studies, L. D. Russell, Lynn Huber, Michael Pregill and James Pace who have been supportive colleagues and welcome conversation partners over the years. Appreciation is also due to Thomas Tiemann, Steven Deloach and Paul Miller who had to endure numerous early morning digressions on Bonhoeffer when they probably just wanted to drink their coffee.

Finally, my deepest gratitude is offered to my wife, Jan Rivero, who has also borne some of the particular struggles of this text. Her encouragement in some difficult days has served as a light on a dark path, not only with this book, but with the journey of life.

ABBREVIATIONS

DBW	*Dietrich Bonhoeffer Works (German)*
DBWE	*Dietrich Bonhoeffer Works (English)*
Ethics	*DBWE*, Vol. 6
GS	*Gesammelte Schriften*
LPP	*Letters and Papers from Prison*
NRS	*No Rusty Swords*

Chapter 1

WHY BONHOEFFER? WHY NOW?

On the west front wall of Westminster Abbey, there is carved a sculpture of modern martyrs. On that wall in stone relief are ten figures that represent martyrs of the twentieth century. Included are such persons as Martin Luther King, Jr, Wang Zhiming of China, Esther John of Pakistan, Grand Duchess Elizabeth of Russia and Archbishop Oscar Romero of El Salvador. Another is Dietrich Bonhoeffer, the German pastor and theologian, who was executed by the Nazis in the last days of their regime. Though some do not believe that Bonhoeffer is a martyr at all and this debate is an interesting one, his presence there marks the impact of his story on the recent history of Christianity.[1]

His image, etched in stone in London, is not the only manifestation of Bonhoeffer that keeps his memory alive. There are also the books still being written about him, academic societies devoted to studying his life and translating his works, and other plays, documentaries and study groups that are testimony to the enduring power of his legacy. He intrigues us for many reasons. One of these reasons is, of course, that Bonhoeffer lived in one of the most difficult times of recent memory. So much was at stake for the world when Bonhoeffer was struggling in the midst of one of the most evil regimes known to humanity

---

[1] Craig Slane has written an entire book on Bonhoeffer and the issue of martyrdom, *Bonhoeffer as Martyr: Social Responsibility and Modern Christian Commitment* (Grand Rapids, MI: Brazos Press, 2004). The book is an examination of the issue that Bonhoeffer is not seen as a religious martyr in some circles because his martyrdom was for political reasons. After a careful examination of martyrdom in Christian history Slane argues that Bonhoeffer as martyr opens up interpretive paths of his theology, especially his *Ethics*, for further consideration. For those readers who are interested in the figures on the wall of martyrs they can consult Andrew Chandler, ed., *The Terrible Alternative: Christian Martyrdom in the Twentieth Century* (London: Cassell, 1998).

to define what it meant to be a Christian, and what Christianity itself looked like.

It seemingly was a time of real absolutes, both good and evil, where the future of the world really was at stake, though these absolutes became more apparent in the aftermath of the war. The ironic part is that those who believed they were truly on the side of the angels, a rather large part of the German Christian church, who were told that they were acting on behalf of God and country, are now seen in our present day as being complicit in barbarism. It is a source of great discomfort to many that they did not fight when they had the chance. But, then again, in times of war every side is told by their governments that they are on God's side. And if you see your government and culture as being on the righteous side you usually have not developed the resources to question which way the world is going.

This was seen most recently in the run-up to the Iraq war when persons from all sides of the theological and political spectrum were employing Bonhoeffer for their arguments, both for and against the war. Most notably, one of George Bush's speechwriters inserted Bonhoeffer's name into two speeches on Iraq and the war on terror. In a special session of the Bundestag in Germany, Bush called Bonhoeffer 'one of the greatest Germans of the 20th century'. He went on to speak of how he gave his life as a witness to the Gospel of life, and 'paid the cost of his discipleship'.[2]

This would not be the only time the president would invoke Bonhoeffer either. He also referred to Bonhoeffer in a commencement speech at Concordia University Wisconsin, where he addressed the Abu Ghraib prisoner abuse scandal and called it the failure of a few bad characters. He asserted that the behaviour of one person can show the character of a whole country in the hour of testing and then gave Bonhoeffer as just such an example, quoting his observation that 'The Church is the Church only when it exists for others'.[3]

Bush was not the only one who was using Bonhoeffer to make arguments about how to respond to terror. The blogosphere was intensely used to mount arguments both pro and con regarding the war in Iraq.[4]

---

[2] Transcript: 'President Bush Thanks Germany for Support Against Terror,' delivered at the Bundestag (Berlin, Germany), found at http://www.whitehouse.gov/news/releases/2002/05/print/20020523-2.html, accessed 14 July 2008. This citation and some of the other websites to follow are taken from Robert O. Smith's unpublished paper, 'Bonhoeffer, Bloggers, and Bush: Uses of a "Protestant Saint" in the Fog of War.'

Most of the arguments using Bonhoeffer were definitely arguing for removal of Hussein and justified their arguments by showing that sometimes war was justified to protect people from a tyrant such as Saddam Hussein and this was a last resort to protect the Iraqi people. One blogger, Martin Roth, succinctly summed up his argument with the show-stopper: 'hands up all the Christians who think Dietrich Bonhoeffer was wrong to try and kill Adolf Hitler?'[5] His was not the only voice relying on Bonhoeffer for justification to prosecute the war against the Iraqi regime.[6]

The Iraq war, however, occurs in a larger context that presently drives much of the world. Though this has been framed as part of the 'war on terror', the historical roots of the conflicts that disturb the Middle East are unknown to most because we have not done enough work to understand the long train of events that have brought us to the present difficulties. To study the various causes of the present conflict would reveal the complicity of the West in the affairs of countries that benefited from the West's needs for energy and the resentment this bred among the disenfranchised of those countries.

These are complex stories and it is not the purpose of this text to exhaustively analyse the historical reasons for our present situation. But this is the context within which we read Bonhoeffer and if he is to serve as a justification to action for some in present circumstances we should be aware of the ways in which he is being used. We should also

---

[3] Transcript: 'President Bush's Concordia Commencement Speech,' *Milwaukee Journal Sentinel*, 14 May 2004, available at www.jsonline.com/news/oswash/may04/229423.asp, accessed 14 July 2008. Of course, as later events regarding torture are still unfolding as of this book, the corruption and corrosion involved in torture of other human beings is revealing itself to be more widespread than just a couple of bad persons.

[4] For example, a Google search for Dietrich Bonhoeffer war on terror comes up with about 10,700 hits.

[5] Martin Roth, 'Just War, Christians and Iraq – Where is the Justice in Not Attacking?' (29 October 2002), available at www.martinrothonline.com/MRCC36.htm. Quoted from Smith.

[6] In fact, the references to Bonhoeffer were incredibly numerous throughout academic discussions as well. One of the most interesting was a panel at the American Academy of Religion meeting in 2003 where Stanley Hauerwas, Jean Bethke Elshtain and George Hunsinger explored Bonhoeffer and the war on terror. There were obviously three different Bonhoeffer's represented, but Hunsinger, who had the final talk definitely created a stir when he said that he, like Bonhoeffer, prays for the defeat of his country.

be alert to how legitimate the use of Bonhoeffer is when he is employed to argue certain positions.

Does Bonhoeffer have any wisdom for us in the midst of current tensions, other than the appeal to removing tyrants? In the pages that follow I hope to explore some of the things he has to teach us concerning God, religion, patriotism and, most importantly, how Christianity takes shape in the conflict between religion and secularity. One example of the fault lines of our situation is precisely the chasm between those who are fervently and devoutly religious in the faith of Islam and a western world that has been successful in removing religion from the sphere of public influence except in the most superficial ways. In American society, there may be the manifestation of civil religion in governmental affairs, but most often it does not exercise substantial impact on foreign or domestic policy other than to serve the national interests. But, before we take up that examination, perhaps a quick look at some others who lay claim to his legacy would help us understand why Bonhoeffer has affected so many lives.

WHOSE BONHOEFFER?

Bonhoeffer was caught in the tensions of his time, like we all are, and because of that he remains of fascination to many. He has always been a type of spiritual Rorschach test. We read him, or of him, and we find there whatever we hope to find. David Hopper makes the observation that each interpreter of Bonhoeffer finds material to support his or her own interpretation, a blank canvas upon which we portray what we wish to see.[7]

More recently, Stephen R. Haynes has written that in the field of Bonhoeffer studies his life and work have generated a type of cult that has both sanctified Bonhoeffer's memory by making him a saint and has wrongly used Bonhoeffer in applying his life to ours:

> Specifically, the Bonhoeffer cult *domesticates* his legacy by placing it in the service of contemporary questions, needs, and concerns whose connection with his own time and place are sometimes tenuous and often more symbolic than real; and it *sanctifies* the theologian's memory by making criticism of his life and thought seem disrespectful or even sacrilegious.[8]

---

[7] David H. Hopper, *A Dissent on Bonhoeffer* (Philadelphia, PA: Westminster Press, 1975), p. 71.

While it is of some debate as to whether this is true of Bonhoeffer studies altogether, or just one small segment of it, it is without question that Bonhoeffer has been embraced by a number of different theological and ideological perspectives ever since his death. This begs the question, however, of whether his life, thought and example can serve us in the present time without doing violence to him. When everyone from abortion clinic bombers to radical secularists lay claim to his legacy how do we read him in our day without projecting onto him our agendas? Perhaps this is an impossible task, but the fact remains that his life is interpreted and his legacy claimed by different voices.

This legacy was kept in play in the beginning by one of Bonhoeffer's students and friends, Eberhard Bethge. Everyone should have such a friend. Because of Bethge's work, Bonhoeffer is seen by many as a heroic figure of constancy before the utter collapse of Christianity under the Nazis. He becomes our talisman against evil, the one we point to if we are unfamiliar with the history of the time and say, 'Well, at least he stood fast.' This, like all assessments of his life is both yes and no, true and false. The various examinations of his life have indeed given to us several different images of Bonhoeffer to consider.

The Bonhoeffer of the 1960s reflected in no small part the tenor of the times and it is not surprising that he was explored by a host of figures like John A. T. Robinson, Paul van Buren and Thomas Altizer. From their reading of Bonhoeffer the phrase 'the death of God' entered into the consciousness of American society, most notably through the front page of *Time* magazine.[9] Through the rather facile use of Bonhoeffer's prison correspondence, a picture was painted of Bonhoeffer that was distorted, but one result was that a more rigorous examination of Bonhoeffer's entire corpus ensued.

This gave rise to many discussions about the early and late Bonhoeffer, whether or not he had betrayed his faith by actions taken with the conspiracy to assassinate Hitler, how his thinking may have changed and if there was a basic continuity in his writings.[10] The main question to all these explorations of the theologian was where was the truth

---

[8] Stephen R. Haynes, *The Bonhoeffer Phenomenon: Portraits of a Protestant Saint* (Minneapolis, MN: Augsburg Fortress, 2004), xii.

[9] Haynes quotes the remark that the phrase 'the death of God' was the phrase that launched a thousand press releases. Ibid, p. 20.

[10] This is a perennial discussion in Bonhoeffer studies as evidenced by Ralf K. Wüstenberg's detailed work in, *A Theology of Life: Dietrich Bonhoeffer's Religionless Christianity*, trans. Doug Stott (Grand Rapids, MI. MI: W. B. Eerdmans, 1998).

about Bonhoeffer to be found? Are there ideas, concepts, ways of understanding Christian faith itself, coming from Bonhoeffer that were radical and compelling for later generations? Did he anticipate the themes that still occupy theology, or do we domesticate him solely to our agenda? Did he ask questions that are timeless in the sense that every age struggles with how to live Christian faith in its own time?

Those who apply Bonhoeffer to contemporary issues without an account of the differences between his time and ours run the risk of projecting onto him what they wish. Yet, to see him as someone who struggled with his world, and whose discernment led him to opposition when the rest of his society marched lockstep with the masses, offers us some resources to think through what faithfulness might look like in our age. There is also the negative lesson Bonhoeffer offers with his entrance into the conspiracy as he struggled deeply with how he might take some responsibility for what had taken place in Germany. It is a legacy that is more complex the deeper we examine his life.

And here is where one of the great ironies rests, because persons all across the theological spectrum claim Bonhoeffer, believing firmly that his life and witness support their theological and social position. In fact, this diversity of interpretations comes in no small part from the contradictions of Bonhoeffer's life. Was he traitor or patriot, atheist or Christian, pacifist or assassin? These are only some of the more severe dichotomies that one struggles with when they get too close to Bonhoeffer.

These categories are far too oppositional to adequately describe the reality of Bonhoeffer's life, but this is the paradox of his life story. Exhaustive study into his life and thought has not yet resolved many of the contradictions. It was a life of struggle with God and culture cut short by his execution before resolution, and therefore the heritage of Bonhoeffer's life in the church remains conflicted. Bonhoeffer's response to his world took many different forms and depended on the circumstances he found himself in. This diversity of responses has prepared the way for the different claims on his legacy.

It is not surprising that the liberal wing of Christianity claims Bonhoeffer, for in many ways he aligns with their perspective. 'Liberal commentators stress that Bonhoeffer's religious convictions led him to eschew uncritical obedience to his nation and reject theologies that affirmed the state as a direct expression of God's will.'[11] The uneasy connection between patriotism and an unquestioning attitude to

---

[11] Haynes, p. 40.

government that makes liberal sensitivities nervous allows them to see Bonhoeffer's life and thought as providing a great cautionary tale for us in what some claim (and, one suspects, secretly hope) are the beginning years of the 'war on terror'. Others, finding great inspiration in Bonhoeffer's stand for the poor and oppressed, count him as a strong prophetic voice. It was for reasons like these that numerous liberation theologians from many parts of the world found in him an inspirational figure.[12]

What may be more surprising, is that the radical right also claims Bonhoeffer as one of their own. Mike Bray, one of a number of radical anti-abortion activists who engaged in the bombing of abortion clinics, found support for his actions in the life history of Bonhoeffer, especially Bonhoeffer's involvement in the plot to assassinate Hitler. The fact that Bray also cites Reinhold Niebuhr as justification for religiously inspired violence, though, is further evidence that his reading of theology is coloured by a distinct approach concerning the role of the Christian in public life.

It was not just Mike Bray that appealed to Bonhoeffer to justify his actions. Paul Hill, an anti-abortion terrorist actually executed for the murders of a clinic physician and his security guard, was inspired by Bonhoeffer to commit these acts of murder. One particularly telling quote comes from him:

> Before World War II the church in Germany also shrank from resisting the evils of an unjust, oppressive government. Dietrich Bonhoeffer is an example of a church leader who, as an individual, sought to protect innocent life by plotting the death of Hitler. He is now considered a hero and his *Ethics* is used as a college text. A holocaust was going on and no civil leaders arose (they are hard to find under totalitarian rule). Few people today, looking back, would say that the active civil disobedience of that time should have been restrained. We can be certain that the counsel of restraint today will be regretted by those who look back on it in the future.[13]

Those on the conservative side of the political spectrum can also point to Bonhoeffer's writings themselves where he has some very

---

[12] A good example of the various ways this is shown can be found in the book *The Cost of Moral Leadership: The Spirituality of Dietrich Bonhoeffer* by Geffrey B. Kelly and F. Burton Nelson (Grand Rapids, MI: W. B. Eerdmans, 2003). The authors, drawing on numerous sources, cover a lot of territory in showing the prophetic and liberative dimensions of Bonhoeffer's life.

[13] Paul J. Hill, 'Should We Defend Born and Unborn Children with Force?' (July 1993) at http://www.webcom.com/~pinknoiz/right/knowenemy.html.

decidedly conservative positions regarding gender relations, and in his
Ethics he has some very interesting things to say about the necessity
to protect life in all its forms from those who would eradicate the sick,
the helpless and yes, the unborn.[14]

It is interesting when the liberal and conservative theological perspectives come to something in Bonhoeffer's life like the conversionary moment that he experienced in 1931/1932, the different
interpretations makes one wonder if all theology is ultimately ideology.
Bethge in his biography of Bonhoeffer alludes to this conversionary
moment by commenting that this experience seemed to deepen an
aspect of Bonhoeffer's life that was profoundly personal, and that he
speaks of it as discovering the Bible and becoming a Christian. From
Bonhoeffer's own mouth: 'Then something happened, something that
has changed and transformed my life to the present day. For the first
time I discovered the Bible . . . I had often preached, I had seen a
great deal of the church spoken and preached about it, but I had not
yet become a Christian.'[15]

The interpreter who takes this event in Bonhoeffer's life as a claim
to the evangelical experience today and then moves from this to a later
justification for violence against what he or she sees as immorality in
society does not pay attention to the results of this conversionary
moment in Bonhoeffer's life. Through moments like this, Bonhoeffer
came to believe that the Sermon on Mount should hold a central
place in his theology: 'I believe I know that inwardly I shall be clear
and honest with myself only if I truly begin to take seriously the

[14] Dietrich Bonhoeffer, *Ethics*, ed. Clifford Green. trans. Reinhard Krauss, Charles
C. West, and Douglas W. Stott. *Dietrich Bonhoeffer Works*, vol. 6 (Minneapolis: Minn.:
Fortress Press, 2005), hereafter referred to as *Ethics*. For example, there is this quote:

> To kill the fruit in the mother's womb is to injure the right to life that God
> has bestowed on the developing life. Discussion of the question whether a
> human being is already present confuses the simple fact that, in any case,
> God wills to create a human being and that the life of this developing
> human being has been deliberately taken. And this is nothing but a murder.
> (p. 206).

One must keep in mind that in the context that Bonhoeffer was writing the Nazis
had pushed a particular medical agenda that sought to eradicate all forms of life
that were less than perfect and thus the context impacts his sections on the natural
and the unnatural considerably. Even so, quotes like this make it difficult to think of
Bonhoeffer in terms of contemporary liberalism.
[15]. Eberhard Bethge, *Dietrich Bonhoeffer: A Biography*, rev. and ed. Victoria Barnett
(Minneapolis, MN: Fortress Press, 2000), p. 204.

Sermon on the Mount. That is the only source of power capable of blowing up the whole phantasmagoria (i.e. the Nazi illusion) once and for all.'[16] How does a man understand the Sermon on the Mount as having so much power it can stop the Nazi juggernaut and then turn to aiding and abetting assassination to rid his nation of evil? The Sermon on the Mount is hardly an invitation to violence at this point, but why Bonhoeffer turns to desperate measures is only one reason why he is interpreted so diversely.

Also from the right side of the spectrum comes one of the more controversial interpretations of the theologian. Georg Huntemann's book, *The Other Bonhoeffer*, introduces us to another Bonhoeffer than the one commonly incorporated by the left. He writes that Bonhoeffer was forever the aristocratic person. He was born into a certain station in German society and his revolt against Nazism was in order to protect the world he had been born into. 'The aristocratic Bonhoeffer saw in the National Socialist ideology a creature from the deep, an uprising of the masses of the collective, of the ordinary, of rampant disorder.'[17] In this way, Bonhoeffer stood primarily for order and so cannot be hijacked by those who do not share his position: 'No, Bonhoeffer is not a church father of the progressives, the feminists, or the emancipators. He should not be left to the left wing.'[18] He writes that Bonhoeffer will have to be seen as the father of evangelicalism in the contemporary setting, or else they will have no father.

Huntemann goes on to argue that liberalism was responsible for the Church's seduction by Nazism: 'all of the anti-Christian elements of the Nazi period continue to be at work precisely among those who count themselves, often with such careless disregard of history, part of the progressive or left-wing scene.'[19] It is rhetoric such as this that allows some conservative evangelicals such as James C. Dobson, the

---

[16] Ibid.

[17] Georg Huntemann, *The Other Bonhoeffer: An Evangelical Reassessment of Dietrich Bonhoeffer*, trans. Todd Huizinga (Grand Rapids, MI: Baker, 1993), p. 265. The fact that Huntemann can argue this shows in some measure how his prejudices do not allow him a clear perspective for what was going on in Germany at the time. In fact the aristocracy, such as it was, located itself in the economic structure of Germany and they benefited greatly from Hitler being in power. It is true that the conspiracy of those in the military was motivated by aristocratic concerns about the survival of Germany and not the suffering of the Jews, but Bonhoeffer, as aligned with those concerns as it may have seemed, nonetheless had other reasons for his participation.

[18] Ibid., p. 87.

[19] Ibid., p. 11.

founder of Focus on the Family, to appeal to Bonhoeffer as a case study of Christian political activism. The perspective put forth is that Christians constitute an embattled minority living in the midst of a godless and permissive state. One wonders how long this tact can be used when those who represent the forces of the Christian right in American society today actively seek to hold the hands of those who control the levers of political power.

The reality of conflicting interpretations contributes to the issue of whose Bonhoeffer does the least violence to his legacy. In some part, this is determined by which Bonhoeffer's writings one concentrates on. His early theological writings like *Sanctorum Communio* and *Act and Being* are theologically dense and tend to draw little attention among the public, relegated mostly to the realm of scholars and students. It is *Discipleship, Life Together* and *Letters and Papers from Prison* that most people read to learn of Bonhoeffer. And though these all have great and striking power, for the interpreter of Bonhoeffer they offer tensions that make Bonhoeffer so difficult to pigeonhole.

IS BONHOEFFER STILL RELEVANT?

One cannot easily translate Bonhoeffer into our age because the circumstances of his life were much different. We consider those times unique because of the personality of the main actor driving events, Adolf Hitler. We sometimes invoke the name Hitler in our day, if for no other reason than that he has become a fetish, a symbol not only of evil, but of our relationship to it. Because Hitler functions as the absolutization of evil such that no one surpasses him in malignancy, he becomes a symbol that hides a reality we don't want to face – what the Nazi regime represented is not unique in human history and is likely to be replicated on a different scale.

There are governments and political systems that create as much suffering as the National Socialists, though they do not rise to the level of the Holocaust and world war. Since they do not rise to that level they slip being accountable to the larger world community. Because we have no rhetorical ability to speak of evil in any other way but the most horrific personal example we can find, we fail to uncover and reveal the impulses and structural forces of violence and destruction that drive much of the world today. These structural issues can be found in political systems that mirror what the Nazis brought to the world, even if they do not have the specific personality of Hitler at the controls. In this sense, Bonhoeffer can be a source of reflection on contemporary events as long as we are able to see that the same dynamics of power operative in his age are always present in human culture, though they assume different forms in different systems.

But this is not the same as facing the beast in Bonhoeffer's day. He was in the belly of that beast, struggling with the spirit of negation that permeated the Nazi agenda. And because of this struggle, Bonhoeffer still captures our imagination. This prompts us to look more carefully at the way that the society of the National Socialists under Hitler operated to construct the state in their name. Their twin towers of bureaucracy and nationalism became the means by which the state required absolute obedience and brooked no opposition. All worldviews that did not conform were attacked, and confusion about the role of the church and state was debilitating. Our preoccupation with Hitler should not blind us to the reality that what happened to German society can happen anywhere. There is a fragility of all societies to the same forces. No society stands immune from the power of fear invoked to protect us from our 'enemies'.

Seen in this light, Bonhoeffer is not entirely distant from our age. Without vigilance we, too, can become accomplices of darkness. It happens with appeals to the best in people, to our patriotism and love of country, or to the worst in us, our fears of others, or even of death. If these appeals are not critically evaluated and measured, we slide into nationalism and xenophobia. What begins as a promise to restore honour slides into the Manichaean world of 'us' and 'them', the chosen and the infidel. In our time, no less than Bonhoeffer's, those who are cynical corrupt the idealistic. Does Bonhoeffer hold any wisdom for us in the midst of our struggles?

The questions of loyalties and commitments also transcend the context of his day. The issues of who we are, who God is, and how we live in the space between, move us beyond the context of Bonhoeffer's time. The struggles and questions of his time continue to intrigue us because his response to these things was forged in the fiercest of fires. We live in an age when the faith of millions of Americans lacks any historical consciousness, a time when Christianity has become a matter of 'meeting needs' or 'personal salvation', a time of stultifying superficiality. No less than in Bonhoeffer's age the church today faces challenges that go to the very core of what constitutes Christianity, and whether or not it is possible to define what faith in Christ really means in a time of global conflict.

In the pages to come, I intend on exploring the contradictions of Bonhoeffer's life and I hope you will reflect with me on what we are to make of Bonhoeffer in the present age. He does have a perspective that can be disturbing to those whose theology tends to be nothing more than a cloaked political ideology of one sort or the other. The implications I am drawing from his work can be profoundly disturbing. When he is writing about the responsible person in *Ethics*, he warns that the ideologue does not think clearly about his position. Because the demand of ideological purity is so strong, careful and thoughtful consideration for the true results of actions gets lost: 'Those who act on the basis of ideology consider themselves justified by their idea.'[20] Is there wisdom in this observation concerning where American culture finds itself today? For all sides of the political and theological world, it is difficult to claim Bonhoeffer as one's own without acknowledgement that he moves beyond the dichotomous categories of liberal/conservative we are presently stuck in.

READING BONHOEFFER IN TROUBLED TIMES

As mentioned, one cannot easily translate Bonhoeffer into our current age because the circumstances are so much different. And yet, we do live in the 'world come of age' that Bonhoeffer probed from his prison cell and this presents us with deep challenges to think through and live out in the coming years. Bonhoeffer was struggling to give voice to something he saw coming on the horizon, something manifest today in society and the church, but his traditional foundation did not allow him to take the next step. The steps he takes in prison are radical enough, and we will never truly know what may have come next, but he sensed a world ending and something that would change the world waiting in the wings. Maybe in the rubble of the world after Auschwitz, a fresh start for Christianity was needed.

In his day millions of 'God fearing' Christians became accomplices in genocide. It happened step-by-step, law-by-law. It happened for many reasons, but the most disconcerting one was that the religious heritage of Christianity had prepared the way. The results of this are

---

[20] *Ethics*, pp. 225–26. In this particular writing one can see that Bonhoeffer has already moved to another community of action than the church. He writes that because God became human, responsible action must surrender to God the ultimate judgement of good or evil and consider the consequences of the act. The ideologue doesn't even consider the consequences, they just believe in the absoluteness of their ideology. This alone should give us pause when we consider the forces that are driving the present conflict.

tragically apparent in retrospect, but why did so few people see this at the time? What were the cultural forces at work that allowed blatant propaganda to shape reality for so many? Does Bonhoeffer address what happens when a society feels under attack or threatened and capitulates to its fears?

When Bonhoeffer writes in *Discipleship* that Christians must have 'an irresistible love of the downtrodden, the sick, the wretched, the wronged, the outcast and all who are tortured with anxiety', then what does that mean for us today in the shadows of Abu Ghraib?[21] Can we stand by in this moment and justify atrocity and violence in Bonhoeffer's or the state's name? Keith Clements contends that: 'Bonhoeffer's message is not that patriotism always ends in idolatry, but that loyalty to country must include "recognition and acceptance of one's country's guilt, and intercession and action for its expiation."'[22] Who in American society today is taking responsibility for our actions in the world? To even suggest such a thing in the present climate is to risk the charge of treason. Yet we know that the day will come when this responsibility will be taken. History always demands this from humanity. Can Bonhoeffer serve as our guide for this moment?

Take a cold look at the world today, pierce the propaganda, the politics, and if you have the courage you can see beyond the grand schemes of political theory and economic power that are offered by a small cabal of actors as justifications for the 'war on terror'. These are the schemes that make moral validity reducible to political legitimacy and so corrupt a society. What can Bonhoeffer offer us in this moment? Perhaps one thing he can offer us is the realization that when a nation acts in order to secure its own interests at the expense of the oppressed it is an embodiment of sin.

In the midst of our age it is difficult to be able to see with what Miroslav Volf called double vision, the ability to see with God's eyes the life of those on the margins, those on the periphery who bear the brunt of those in the centres of power. Bonhoeffer observes: 'The church confesses that it has witnessed the arbitrary use of brutal force, the suffering in body and soul of countless innocent people, that it has witnessed oppression, hatred, and murder without raising its voice for the victims

---

[21] Dietrich Bonhoeffer, *Discipleship*, ed. Geffrey B. Kelly and John D. Godsey, Dietrich Bonhoeffer Works, vol. 4 (Minneapolis, MN: Fortress Press, 2003), see Haynes, p. 40.

[22] Haynes, pp. 39–40.

and without finding ways of rushing to help them.'[23] Do we need to develop new visions?

For Bonhoeffer, being responsible to his faith meant that patriotism cannot cause us to make one's own culture absolute at the expense of the world, for other lives make their claims on ours. Other's hopes, dreams and aspirations emerge from the shadows and mists of the fog of war to stand in front of us, wounded unto death, and ask 'In whose name do you do these things?'

Bonhoeffer walked that tightrope between embracing the people of his land, the heritage of his land, the promise of his land, while at the same time accepting responsibility for its crimes. It is here that many will take their leave, for you who are reading these pages may think, 'But my nation has committed no crimes to confess, we follow the path of righteousness to restore freedom to the world.' Perhaps Bonhoeffer creates the space for us to step back, gain perspective, and see that those who have political power often claim they possess the purest motives and yet can do great harm in the world.

Secure in their own ideologies, those whose imperial pretensions are built on the self-interests of political hegemony are willing to look at all those individuals who will die at their hands as the indispensable and necessary costs of their new world. Bonhoeffer allows us to see this for what it truly is, the wisdom of expediency masquerading as political realism. Bonhoeffer has another word of confession for us: 'The church confesses that it has looked on silently as the poor were exploited and robbed, while the strong were enriched and corrupted.'[24] From where will the church find a prophetic voice to speak to power about the lives that are destroyed in the wake of its relentless march to control and security?

Some will respond that the church should be intimately involved in the state's agenda, otherwise there is little countervailing force to hold the state to the rule of law. Bonhoeffer himself argues this position at points in his life. Because the government has to be concerned with concrete situations that are life and death in their consequences the church should assume some responsibility, even if it has to get its hands dirty in the process. Bonhoeffer himself believed that this was a legitimate role for the church. In order to save the state from itself, the church must be involved in the larger government of society.

---

[23] *Ethics*, p. 139.
[24] Ibid., 140.

There is a voice that challenges us no less than in Bonhoeffer's day, 'Don't want thousands dead from ethnic cleansing or terrorism? Well, you better not hold to the moral high ground when the necessity for violence becomes unavoidable. If we live in a fallen world and the government is there to restrain evil then the church better think long and hard about its responsibilities. Sometimes the innocent can only be protected by force.' These are difficult questions that are not to be avoided. But what if the state itself becomes the problem? Either way, the church cannot retreat into some private space, secure in its own piety. We cannot evade our responsibility as Christians to contribute to the well being of our nation and the world. So the question Bonhoeffer confronts us with is, what shape does the church take in the present day of conflict?

Or, perhaps, more crucially, whose Christ does the church follow? Bonhoeffer centred all his theology on the figure of Jesus Christ and believed that Christ shared in some measure our sufferings: 'Jesus Christ is not the transfiguration of noble humanity, but the Yes of God to real human beings, not the dispassionate Yes of a judge but [the] merciful Yes of a compassionate sufferer.'[25]

Bonhoeffer understood that for the Christian, God's becoming incarnate in Jesus makes contempt for human beings impossible and the manipulation of them is reprehensible. No appeal to the status of another human being as enemy or infidel is justified in light of God's willingness to assume humanity and mediate forgiveness of sins. It is a contemptuous act to treat others with something other than that divine Yes: 'The despiser of humanity sees mainly the weak, base and mean sides of people and can draw one of two conclusions from this: either to make use of people by appealing to their basest instincts and thereby make them meaner than they already are, or to withdraw in disgust from people and leave them to their own devices.'[26]

Both the liberal and conservative are challenged by this because it means that you cannot use people by appealing to their worst nature, nor should you withdraw and leave them to their own devices. In the

---

[25] Ibid., p. 85.

[26] Ibid. In this section of the *Ethics* Bonhoeffer has a powerful section on the despiser of humanity and one cannot read this unaware of the context within which he is writing. His description of the despiser captures powerfully the political leadership of Hitler. It is a sobering description of what condition German society is acquiring. This quote was found in Bonhoeffer's original working draft, but deleted in order to be expanded in the following pages of this section.

political order today, there are those who would pit persons against one another on the basis of worldviews shaped by religion. They have no great love for humankind because they have already judged without compassion. It is power that interests them, not community. Being pawns in other's desire to maintain power, persons' deepest beliefs are manipulated by those who want of them nothing other than a vote, or perhaps a warm body for the machinery of death and terror they have constructed. Here is the tough part – it is not just 'them', it is also 'us'. This is what attention to Bonhoeffer can offer us – the ability to see beyond a world that the powers in culture have the power to shape in such a way that silences the voices of its victims.

His powers of discernment are in full evidence when he writes: 'That evil appears in the form of light, of beneficence, of faithfulness, of renewal, that it appears in the form of historical necessity, of social justice, is for the commonsense observer a clear confirmation of its profound evilness.'[27] Bonhoeffer goes on to say that how we respond to evil can be deficient because it becomes a matter of misunderstanding its real power.

Inward purity will not do, reasonable people who 'want to be fair to both sides' will fail, fanatics will not succeed because 'Though their fanaticism serves the lofty goals of truth and justice, sooner or later they are caught in small and insignificant things and fall into the net of their more clever opponent.'[28] Evil is too cloaked for us to understand its true nature, and it often appears to us as a historical necessity. We must have this weapon to protect ourselves, we must destroy these people who threaten us; the list is manifold of horrors we have justified.

And usually this means appeal to grand themes and totalizing narratives. This is how we construct our ideologies after all. In our time and world, the modern idea of humanity ever progressing and morally perfectible has collapsed, and it is not coming back. The grand illusions that drove humankind for the last two centuries have eroded in the face of continual violence and war. What will be the new ideologies that will ask of us commitment and perhaps worship at their altars? One does not have to look far for candidates.

One hears much talk of freedom and its handmaiden, democracy, as candidates for containing the aspirations of humankind. But, there lurks the suspicion that this is the rhetoric to mask a broader and more

---

[27] Ibid., 77.
[28] Ibid., 78.

banal force – economic consumerism. What is not being noticed by so many is how we are shaped as persons by the vulgarity of consumerism. We become enchanted with the superficial, defined by the fashion of the time or the amount we have accumulated. Do we seek to define ourselves by love of wisdom or the growth of character that is shaped by the compassion of others learned only by the experience of suffering? In a world of such relentless forces, does Bonhoeffer offer any wisdom?

Religion also stakes a claim to the allegiances of many. The forms it takes are varied, and it can easily show its deadly and coercive sides even within religions that are ostensibly of peace (though no religion I am aware of has said they are for war). Because of the power of religion to define the deepest identity of persons, we find in religion the attempt to manipulate, control and co-opt divine transcendence in service of the ideologies of power. When Bonhoeffer addresses the issue of religionless Christianity, is he trying to escape a certain gravity that pulls all human religions into its orbit? How does God become understood as something other than a tribal deity that we wrap in a national flag and send out to war? This, too, is a place where Bonhoeffer may offer a voice of discernment for us and especially for those who call themselves Christian.

In the context of Bonhoeffer's life, we see the manifestation of one of Western Christianity's greatest failures. Its inability to dissociate itself from the military and political apparatus of Nazi Germany, its unwillingness to cultivate a strong prophetic voice, its betrayal of its own faith; all these things serve to illustrate that Christianity in that situation had become nothing more than an enfeebled and useless religion. Though there were pockets of resistance, these were a minority.

Bonhoeffer's struggles with this environment are guides to us of how difficult it is to define faith in the midst of such moral confusion. Larry Rasmussen alludes to this when he writes of how Bonhoeffer moved from the prophetic witness and moral certainty of *Discipleship* to a place where the moral uncertainty and social chaos of Germany were reflected in *Ethics*, and *Letters and Papers from Prison*. In his struggles, Bonhoeffer seeks to bring to light a different way of understanding Christian faith than had previously been known.[29]

---

[29] See Larry Rasmussen, *Dietrich Bonhoeffer's Significance for North American Christians* (Philadelphia, PA: Fortress Press, 1990), p. 52. Also, see Rasmussen's book, *Dietrich Bonhoeffer: Reality and Resistance* (Nashville, TN: Abingdon Press, 1972). This has just been reissued by Westminster/John Knox Press.

The cultural captivities that pass as substitutes for faith in God presently constitute ample evidence of how deeply we need new ways of understanding what Christianity is for us today. This book examines a number of these issues in the coming chapters, using Bonhoeffer as both guide and foil. I will explore these questions because I think Bonhoeffer's greatest contribution to us was that he asked the right questions.

Towards the end of his life, Bonhoeffer wrote from prison that he would like to write a book when he got out. It was to be a short book, not more than a 100 pages, divided into three chapters. In the first chapter, he intended to take stock of Christianity. He would examine humankind's coming of age and the attendant religionlessness of a humanity that had no need of God to order its affairs. In the second chapter, he was going to explore the question of God and how God was to be talked about in the 'world come of age'. In the final chapter, he was going to address the life of the church and its existence for others rather than itself.[30] In this book, Bonhoeffer was intending to raise questions that had pressed themselves upon him with particular urgency. In some ways, this is my attempt to follow his outline; a stock-taking of Christianity and the world in which we presently find ourselves and what the contours of a faithful witness to the gospel of Jesus Christ might look like in today's circumstances.

There are some things we face today though, that, while different, share the same family resemblances. We stand in a perilous moment in the history of the world. Circumstances have thrust us into a situation where many are calling for a struggle that will last for our foreseeable lifetimes. When government officials use the term 'long war', they are seeking to shape reality in such a way that all the social and political life of the human family will oscillate around concerns that they control. This may not be a conscious decision, because many feel they are just responding to events on the ground, but this is the way that reality gets shaped nonetheless. Every event will be interpreted as a part of that particular narrative, and the very framing of the world becomes closed to other possibilities.

This was much the way it was in Germany in the early 1930s. Just like then, the world is shaped by economic and cultural forces to construct our exterior and interior worlds in such a way that we no longer

[30] Dietrich Bonhoeffer, *Letters and Papers from Prison*, ed. Eberhard Bethge (New York, NY: Macmillan, 1975), pp. 380–83. Hereafter cited as *LPP*.

have the imagination left to construct a different world. How much different would the world look today if back in 1932 the Christians of Germany had engaged in civil resistance to all forces that sought to demonize other human beings and fed upon the fears of a defeated population?

There is much to deal with now, but one question I am haunted by is how will we be understood 50 years from now? Will there be a shaking of the head and the same kind of disappointment that we feel when we look back at Bonhoeffer's day? Where is the Christian faith being held captive to ideology and political seduction? How does the church exist for others today, or does it? And most central to this book will be the question, what is Christianity for us today? These are the types of concerns that are always contemporaneous and why we will never be done with Bonhoeffer. He stands as witness to those who have the courage to ask such questions in the middle of a society that is blinded and self-deceived. We ought to be asking such questions, and Bonhoeffer can help us in the task at hand. We turn now to a brief synopsis of his life.

Chapter 2

A LIFE AMONG THE FRAGMENTS

There was nothing that would have indicated early in his life that Dietrich Bonhoeffer would become one of the world's most famous theologians. His was a family of successful and accomplished people in German society that offered him all the privileges afforded to someone of his social position. Born 4 February 1906, with his twin sister Sabine, he would grow up surrounded by family and haunted by the death of his brother. Christianity was of a conventional sort in his house, something to be acknowledged and invited in at special occasions and cultural holidays, but not a vital part of the family. The Bonhoeffer family moved to Berlin in 1912 when Dietrich's father, Karl, accepted the leading professorship for psychiatry and neurology in Germany.

From here the family would experience the horrors of World War I, where Dietrich lost one of his brothers, and its aftermath, which even to a well-off family was a dreadful trial. Bonhoeffer recounted the impact of this in an address to an American audience where he tried to describe the reality of what hunger and deprivation did to many in Germany and how this helped in no small way to prepare the way for what was to follow.[31]

It is difficult to know for sure what made Bonhoeffer choose the path he did in life.[32] It was a way of marking independence from his

---

[31] This address is found in the book *No Rusty Swords: Swords, Letters, Lectures, and Notes, 1928–1936, from the Collected Works of Dietrich Bonhoeffer,* vol. I, ed. Edwin H. Robertson, trans. Edwin H. Robinson and John Bowden (New York, NY: Harper and Row, 1965), pp. 76–85. Hereafter cited as *NRS*.

[32] Bethge in recounting Bonhoeffer's career decisions says that even this was hidden in some respects because of Bonhoeffer's concern that one's innermost vocation should remain hidden. Bethge, p. 34.

brothers and the rest of the family, but also, as we reflect on it, it is perhaps a mystery to be pondered that our lives do indeed manifest a calling in them that cannot be accounted for solely by our family.

Bonhoeffer started his theological training in the usual places of German education and was schooled by the names that have become connected with Protestant liberalism, Reinhold Seeberg, Karl Holl and most famously, Adolf von Harnack. Sometime around the end of 1924 and the beginning of 1925, Bonhoeffer discovered Karl Barth, a theologian that fired his intellectual neurons. It was here he would be introduced to dialectical theology. This would be a relationship that would grow and develop over the years as the two became involved in very different ways with what was happening in Germany.

In 1927, he completed his initial dissertation, which was later hailed by Karl Barth as a theological miracle. This work, *Sanctorum Communio*, would deal with themes that would continue throughout Bonhoeffer's life. It is here where he works out his initial ideas of 'person' and the ethical relation to the 'other'. He investigates the social intention of Christian concepts and seeks to develop his ecclesiology in a profoundly christocentric way, centring everything on the form that Jesus Christ assumes in the concrete moment. These early theological concepts would find expression throughout the rest of his life, impacting Bonhoeffer's thoughts and ideas about the relation of the divine and the human and the social expression of God and humankind.

Though it would have seemed that he was well on his way to becoming a quintessential German theologian of the early twentieth century, following in the steps of Harnack, Bonhoeffer decided to take a pastoral appointment in Barcelona where some of his formative ideas and concepts found concrete expression in pastoral formation. He was able to experience a great deal of Spain and its people from his base in Barcelona, but he was committed to his pastoral duties as well.[33] More interestingly, he was exploring the themes that would mark his theological work later on. Central among these were the role of Christianity as a manifestation of religion, the 'provincialism' to which Christ's church had succumbed, and who the 'real' Jesus was.[34]

This narrowing down of Jesus into one who has been totally captivated by culture usually ends with Christ serving the parochial interests

---

[33] Ibid., pp. 98–105.

[34] Ibid., pp. 113–20. He was not entirely able to overcome that provincialism himself though as is evident from some of his writings from this time.

of a particular society, but not the larger interest of God's reign. Even at this point in his life, though, Bonhoeffer was seeking ways to unmask what he understood as religion so that faith may find its correct expression.

In 1929, he returned to Berlin to take up academic work once more, finishing his second dissertation, *Act and Being*. During this time, groups that were highly nationalistic and who had suffered and chafed under the restrictions imposed on Germany in the aftermath of World War I were beginning to assert themselves in German society. They appealed to a felt and perceived injustice that had positioned Germany in difficult circumstances. As part of their agenda, they denounced any attempts at the type of international co-operation that might have aided Germany as foreign efforts to enslave the German people.[35] This nascent political movement sought to isolate Germany, arguing that no one should be allowed to tell Germany what to do and above all, no national sovereignty should be conceded to any international forces. Anyone who disagreed with this perspective was charged as 'unpatriotic'.[36]

As this was taking place, the world experienced economic difficulties brought about by the Great Depression. This only exacerbated the tensions within Germany as the right wing bourgeoisie's clamour for a more authoritarian hand began to grow louder. As in most of these moments, the forces of authoritarianism found plenty of enemies to aim at in their desire to find a scapegoat for their difficulties. It came as little surprise that the Jewish people would end up on the receiving end of this hatred.

Though Bonhoeffer was not totally oblivious to these rising strains of fascism, he was absorbed in the academic demands of *Act and Being*. This work, which would mark his academic career in significant ways, was dealing with the issue of how God's being was God's action. He was exercised by theological and epistemological questions in this text and wrote it in conversation with both philosophy and theology. Some of the ideas expressed in this text would find their way into Bonhoeffer's 'nonreligious' interpretation later on.

In the second half of 1929, another idea emerged which would have a profound impact on Bonhoeffer's life, the suggestion that he go to America as an exchange student. In preparation for this trip, he

---

[35] Ibid., pp. 125–26.
[36] Ibid.

reviewed the history of Germany and the aftermath of the war. Some of these studies would find their way into remarks he made to American audiences about the deprivation that Germany faced after the war.[37]

Bonhoeffer's visit to the United States and his stay at Union Theological Seminary in New York City would open up new worlds to him that would have lasting impact on the rest of his life. Some of this influence was to be found in the friends he made. One of the most important was Erwin Sutz from Switzerland who helped Bonhoeffer adjust to his environment, but also served as the conduit for bringing Bonhoeffer and Karl Barth together. Sutz and Bonhoeffer had the natural rapport of serious theological students who spoke the same language.

Another European who would also become influential in Bonhoeffer's life was Jean Lasserre, a Frenchman, who Bonhoeffer had a difficult time connecting with in the beginning.[38] Lasserre, at least, was serious about theology and knew more of Bonhoeffer's world than the Americans did. It was Lasserre who confronted Bonhoeffer with the peace commandment of Jesus and pushed Bonhoeffer on the issue of pacifism. Bethge writes about this impact:

> Not that Bonhoeffer immediately became a convinced pacifist – in fact he never did so – but after meeting Lasserre the question of the concrete reply to the biblical injunction of peace and of the concrete steps to be taken against warlike impulses never left him again.[39]

Out of these challenges, Bonhoeffer looked more closely at the Sermon on the Mount and its impact on Christian discipleship, thoughts which ultimately found expression in *Discipleship*.

Bonhoeffer also made friends with Americans as well, most notably the African American student, Frank Fisher. Through his relationship with Fisher, Bonhoeffer came into contact with the racism of the country, but he also came into contact with a vital part of American church life represented by the Abyssinian Baptist Church in Harlem.

[37] *NRS*, pp. 78–83. Bonhoeffer says some profound things about what war can do to a country's psyche and the impact upon society. There are sobering words in this address for anyone who has suffered the results of war, or anybody who unleashes it upon a population.

[38] Bethge, pp. 153–54. Bethge attributes this to the fact that Germans still had lingering feelings of resentment towards the French in the aftermath of the war.

[39] Ibid., p. 153.

Bonhoeffer committed to worship at Abyssinian and in turn learned much about the problem of race in America.

Finally, Bonhoeffer would find a home away from home in the house of Paul and Marion Lehmann. Paul Lehmann understood Europe and could understand why Bonhoeffer found the theological situation at Union so exasperating. In Bonhoeffer's opinion, American students just didn't take theology seriously and when they laughed at some of Luther's comments in *De servo arbitrio* Bonhoeffer was thoroughly disgusted.[40] Still, Bonhoeffer tried to find the positive aspects of his life among the students at Union and did take some things away from his first visit to America. In the meantime, the shadows were growing larger in Germany as the National Socialists were making headway in their quest for the levers of power in German political circles.

SHATTERING THE ALREADY BROKEN

When Bonhoeffer returned to Germany in 1931, the political situation had indeed changed. The nationalists were making their voices heard, even to the point of violence on the streets and universities, and fissures were developing that would soon plunge the world into chaos. Bonhoeffer took up his duties as a lecturer at the University of Berlin, but not before a trip to Bonn to meet Karl Barth. This would begin a relationship that would contain tensions and support for them both.[41] Of prime importance to Bonhoeffer was the concrete form the church took in the world. What should it say in the present situation?

It was also during this time that Bonhoeffer entered the orbit of the ecumenical movement by his participation in a conference in Cambridge. This would mark the beginning of a significant interest

[40] *NRS,* p. 91. Bonhoeffer's observations on American Christianity are fascinating to read today in light of subsequent history. His perspective can show that freedom as a free-floating concept can become idolatrous in the current circumstances. We are only free where the Gospel makes room and space for itself precisely where no such freedom exists. As an institutional possession, freedom, is not even an essential mark of the church, pp. 104–05.

[41] One of the most interesting aspects of this relationship is that Barth never really read the first two major works of Bonhoeffer until after his death. It was upon reading *Sanctorum Communio* after Bonhoeffer's death that Barth declared it a theological miracle, not least because it was written in the heart of Protestant liberalism, Berlin. Karl Barth, *Church Dogmatics* III/4 (Edinburgh, UK: T & T Clark, 1958), p. 641.

for Bonhoeffer, an interest that would make him suspect to those who were fearful of any positive relationships with the world that had imposed such hardships on Germany. This led to a backlash against ecumenical work that would weaken the church's response to the National Socialists.[42] The right wing forces of Germany at the time sought to isolate Germany and its citizens, the better to feed their resentment.

It was about this time that we also encounter in Bonhoeffer's life the conversionary moment referred to earlier in Chapter 1. This event had profound implications for how Bonhoeffer understood the Sermon on the Mount. Speaking of his own sense of self-righteousness he wrote: 'Then the Bible, and in particular the Sermon on the Mount freed me from that. Since then everything has changed.'[43] Of some interest in this is the fact that Bonhoeffer came to a new understanding about pacifism. The pacifism he had so opposed he now saw as self-evident, though it is an open question as to whether or not Bonhoeffer himself was ever a pacifist.[44] Though we still have no definitive explanation of what this moment was in Bonhoeffer's life, it appeared to mean that Bonhoeffer's orientation was shifted slightly with the personal appropriation of faith.

Of particular note was a letter he wrote to his brother, Karl-Friedrich, in January of 1935 quoted earlier in the first chapter. In this letter Bonhoeffer considers a renewed interest in the Sermon on the Mount as the only source of power to stand against the Nazi illusion. He says he realizes he may seem fanatical, but theology itself had become different for him, something more personal.[45]

---

[42] See, Bethge, pp. 193–202.

[43] Ibid., p. 205. Bonhoeffer writes that what he had been freed from was making the doctrine of Jesus Christ 'into something of personal advantage for myself . . ..'

[44] Ibid. The relationship of Bonhoeffer to pacifism is one of the most complex aspects of his life. Bethge maintains that he never was a pacifist. Larry Rasmussen in his book, *Reality and Resistance*, argues that Bonhoeffer's commitment to pacifism was situational and provisional. Thus, the issue of whether Bonhoeffer ever advocated a rigorous pacifism is up for question. Rasmussen believes that Bonhoeffer was so deeply concerned about any absolutization of a theological perspective, even pacifism must be always provisional to the moment. Regardless, Rasmussen does point to something profoundly important and that is that whatever attraction pacifism may have had for Bonhoeffer emerged from a theology of the cross and not naiveté about what humankind is capable of. See his discussion, pp. 94–126.

[45] Bethge, p. 205.

When Bonhoeffer began his duties at the University of Berlin, most of the students were attracted to the Nazi ideology. This made for no small challenge in some respects, but Bonhoeffer continued his theological growth through the lectures he gave these students in the context of the political changes that were taking place around him. In these months there were indications that Bonhoeffer was developing the initial formulations of later themes by his continuing attention to the connection between Christology and the church. This would constitute the high point of his academic life in the accepted corridors of German education.

In the background of his life, the momentum for the Nazis was growing in Germany as swastikas were entering the churches and the 'German Christians' were gaining power in Berlin church elections. Bonhoeffer was not unaware of all this, but he was not as yet in the thick of it. When Franz von Papen became Reich chancellor, many people believed that the new Christian conservative government would restore some measure of stability to the situation in Germany. This government invoked God's name in defence of its legitimacy, a move that Bonhoeffer addressed in a sermon on 12 June 1932 when he preached, 'Or is there not concealed behind our religious trends our ungovernable urge toward . . . power – in the name of God to do what *we* want, and in the name of the Christian worldview to stir up and play off one people against another?'[46]

But this government was to pale in comparison to what lay on the horizon. At noon on 30 January 1933, Hitler took over the reins of power from Hindenburg and the shadows extended themselves. The life of a professor or country pastor was forever closed to Bonhoeffer as the situation he and his country found themselves in would, for Bonhoeffer and very few others, demand action and resistance. That the resistance was not more widespread is one of history's tragedies.

Bonhoeffer's resistance took almost immediate form on 1 February as he found himself in front of a microphone on a Berlin radio station to deliver an address on the concept of the *Führer*. It is not exactly clear, how the invitation to give this address occurred, but he was responding from a position of social and cultural conservatism in this speech that nonetheless warned of the dangers of elevating leaders to the place of idols.[47] His speech was cut off before he could finish in what was a foreshadowing of the great propaganda machine to come.

[46] Ibid., p. 236.
[47] Bethge, p. 260.

This rise to power on the part of Hitler was welcomed in many parts of the country in no small part because the Nazis knew how to stoke the resentments and injuries of millions of Germans. Hitler also knew how to appeal to the religious sentiments of his country:

> The national government will maintain and defend the foundations on which the power of our nation rests. It will offer strong protection to Christianity as the very basis of our collective morality. Today Christians stand at the very heart of our country. We want to fill our culture again with the Christian spirit. We want to burn out all the recent immoral developments in literature, in the theater, and in the press – in short, we want to burn out the poison of immorality which has entered our whole life and culture as a result of liberal excess during the past years.[48]

The resulting chaos from Hitler's ascension spilled into the streets of Germany, resulting in ever more repressive measures to keep order. This ferment reached its nadir with the Reichstag fire, setting in motion an overwhelming series of laws passed to help Hitler cement power. The tinder for the fire had been growing given the resentment of many in Germany amid the continuing financial hardships of the global market and the aftermath of the Treaty of Versailles, but now the fire was burning brightly with the rekindled dreams of people who believed, falsely, they were on the verge of a new national era of freedom.

The laws which were passed in such quick succession set the stage for the loss of all personal rights protected by the constitution, established the basis for the construction of concentration camps for the enemies of the state, and initiated a vast network of spying and censorship. It was the initial act of the 'Reichstag Fire Edict' that would provide the political means for the Confessing Church seminary at Finkenwalde to be closed four and a half years later.[49] These laws created the conditions in Germany which made open resistance a crime against the state and, with the Enabling Act, meant that Hitler was not accountable to any legal or constitutional requirement. Soon the laws against the Jews would be passed and the slide into darkness would accelerate. And, in all of this, Hitler faced a compliant church. Large segments of the German Christians began to make their peace

[48] This comes from a radio address that Hitler gave on July 22, 1933. This can be found in *The Speeches of Adolf Hitler, 1922–1939*, vol. 1, Norman H. Baynes, ed. (London: Oxford University Press, 1942), pp. 871–72

[49] Bethge, p. 265.

with this government and in turn sell their soul for the hope that they would be able to have influence in society.

RESISTANCE?

In effect the Protestant Church in Germany became a Reich church, and in this situation the 'Jewish question' emerged to take centre stage. The war on the Jews had begun, and the Christian church in Germany had no real level of resistance to it, and such resistance as was mounted was ineffective. Bonhoeffer himself addressed this issue with an address entitled 'The Jewish Question'. In this address, Bonhoeffer argued that the state is an order of God's preservation in a godless world and thus the state's actions remain free from the church's intervention, but this does not mean that the church lets political action slip by disinterestedly either.[50]

In fact, Bonhoeffer laid out different responses that the church can take vis-à-vis the state, when it acts. One of these is to question the state, another is to aid the victims of state action and the third contains a phrase that became strongly connected with Bonhoeffer: 'The third possibility is not just to bandage the victims under the wheel, but to put a spoke in the wheel itself.'[51] This image of sticking a log in the wheels of the state, of engaging in action that would cause damage to the state's ongoing assault of people in a society, has been invoked several times, most notably by those who resisted the practice of apartheid in South Africa.[52]

Bonhoeffer goes on in this address to say some remarkable things about the relationship of Jews and Christians, things read today with a sense of dismay. He argues on behalf of the Jews not as Jews, but for the Jew who has been baptized. His main concern in this was Christianized Jews like his friend Franz Hildebrandt and brother-in-law Gerhard Leibholz. His remarks on Jews as Jews in this address appear far more ambivalent and in some places offensive to contemporary ears, especially the remarks about the Jews being responsible for the death of Christ and receiving the curse of God in return for their

---

[50] *NRS*, pp. 224–25.

[51] Ibid., p. 225.

[52] See, for example, John W. de Gruchy, *Bonhoeffer and South Africa: Theology in Dialogue* (Grand Rapids, MI: W. B. Eerdmans, 1984).

refusal of Jesus.[53] This address has led to no little interest in how effective the resistance to Hitler was on the part of the church if they could not fight for those who were not Christian and were persecuted by the regime.[54]

Thus was to begin a long struggle with the Nazis on many fronts, a struggle that was as ineffective as it was well intentioned. The purge of the universities was proceeding apace with professors attacked for their 'liberal' views and any new chair was filled with those who would do the regime's business. In the churches, the German Christians were adroitly moving to consolidate political power from within the church. This led to the formation of groups that tried to mount a resistance such as the Young Reformation Movement, of which Bonhoeffer became a part. The precariousness of the situation though continued to be made manifest by such declarations as this from Ludwig Müller: 'All those who are concerned for the safe structure of our church in the great revolution of these times, must . . . feel deeply thankful that the state should have assumed, in addition to all its tremendous tasks, the great load and burden of reorganizing the church.'[55] In the face of such sentiments, the opposition faced no small obstacle.

In July of 1933, the German Christians took over control of Bonhoeffer's church, the Old Prussian Union, and proposed that the Aryan Paragraph, removing Jews from all positions of leadership, become church law. Bonhoeffer opposed this move by means of circulating

---

[53] *NRS*, p. 226.

[54] See, for example, the book *Betrayal: German Churches and the Holocaust* edited by Robert P. Ericksen and Susannah Heschel (Minneapolis, MN: Fortress Press, 1999). This contains a series of essays which question the role of the church in the Hitler regime. There is one essay on Bonhoeffer written by Kenneth C. Barnes entitled, 'Dietrich Bonhoeffer and Hitler's Persecution of the Jews' that is of particular interest. His main argument is that Bonhoeffer contradicts himself even within the essay 'The Church and the Jewish Question.' Barnes argues that for each argument that Bonhoeffer offers for church resistance he presented a counter-argument that negated the first call to action. More recently Stephan R. Haynes has followed up his initial book on Bonhoeffer's reception in the West with another look at Bonhoeffer from a post-Holocaust perspective placing Bonhoeffer carefully in his context and arguing that the legacy Bonhoeffer leaves is complicated. Stephen R. Haynes, *The Bonhoeffer Legacy: Post-Holocaust Perspectives* (Minneapolis, MN: Augsburg Fortress, 2006). Bonhoeffer himself had a moment of personal weakness concerning this issue when Leibholz asked him to conduct the funeral services of his father. His superiors advised him against conducting a funeral for a Jew and he heeded the advice. This was a decision that he deeply regretted and asked Leibholz for forgiveness. Bethge, pp. 275–76.

[55] Ibid., p. 290.

writing in opposition to this, which led in turn to he and Hermann Sasse being given the task of drafting a statement in response to these affairs. They met in August that year at Bethel and wrote a statement that sought to distinguish the authentic tradition of the church from the insipid theology of someone like Müller who reduced Christianity to trust in God and being good.

In the confession written at Bethel, the authors (Bonhoeffer and Sasse were joined by others) sought not only to address the Jewish question, but to offer a robust theology that would rebut all the heresies under which the church was being smothered. There may have been too many heresies to adequately treat, because when the Bethel Confession came before the delegating body the document was watered down significantly, to the point where Bonhoeffer refused to sign it. This signalled Bonhoeffer's slow departure from a church that compromised itself with the state and slighted the racial oppressions that the state was beginning to place on the society.

Bonhoeffer's worst fears were realized when following the take over of the church in July, the Brown synod met in Berlin in September to implement the Aryan Paragraph. Franz Hildebrandt, newly ordained in July, would lose his job under the new law and others would suffer deeply. Bonhoeffer wondered whether to stay in the church or leave and Barth advised him to wait. A statement was drafted that set the situation in the starkest possible terms and most people understood that schism was the only response at this point. From these events was born the Pastors' Emergency League, the first organized dissent against the Nazis' increasing control of the church.[56]

The picture of events in Germany was being portrayed by state supporters differently outside the country thus ensuring that there were conflicting interpretations offered to the outside world. Bonhoeffer attended an ecumenical conference in Sofia, Bulgaria in September of 1933 and gave quite another account of events in Germany. He was able to meet privately with many of the key figures of this conference and alert them to the situation in Germany from his perspective. The Sofia conference produced a resolution that was stinging in its

---

[56] Ibid., pp. 293–311. The reader is encouraged to read Bethge's account of this because his detail of what was taking place behind the scenes can be instructive for understanding how the levers of state power can operate in a coercive fashion. In these months, the Gestapo was very active in this struggle threatening Bonhoeffer and those who aided him. Bonhoeffer himself was told that a concentration camp visit was not outside the realm of possibility, p. 296.

assessment of the implementation of the Aryan clause, which would have ramifications in Germany.

Returning from Sofia, Bonhoeffer arrived in time to attend the national synod in Wittenberg to which he brought a number of pamphlets to be distributed. This synod would also be a disaster for those like Bonhoeffer. This debacle was complete when over Luther's tomb in the church of Wittenberg Castle Joachim Hossenfelder, an impulsive young pastor who would become the German Christian's national leader in 1933, proclaimed: 'I greet thee my Reich Bishop!'[57] This pretty much describes the prospects of a church that sought to find a place of faithfulness to Jesus Christ. After distributing his pamphlets that sought to call into question the direction the church was taking, Bonhoeffer left feeling defeated. In October, he wrote to Barth from London: 'I felt that I was incomprehensibly in radical opposition to all my friends, that my views of matters were taking me more and more into isolation, although I was and remained in the closest personal relationship with these men — and all that made me anxious, made me uncertain.'[58]

Perhaps these words give some clue to Bonhoeffer's inner state and the reasons why he took his next step, leaving Germany to serve parishes in London. His exchange with Barth on this is revelatory of his state of mind, even to the point of not letting Barth know about this until he had left. Barth's response to Bonhoeffer was unsettling in that he did not let Bonhoeffer off easily for leaving Germany and going to London.[59]

Bonhoeffer's stay in London would bring him into contact with a host of figures that would play a role later in his life, including the Anglican bishop of Chichester, George Kennedy Allen Bell, whom he knew from his earlier work in the ecumenical movement and who would become Bonhoeffer's advocate later in helping him interpret to the outside world what was taking place in Germany. Bonhoeffer was in constant contact with the situation back home during his time in London and had to fight the efforts of the Nazi party in London to win adherents to their side. German Christian leaders sought speaking engagements in London and the rest of the United Kingdom, but these were not particularly successful in persuading their audiences that they represented an authentic Christian witness in Germany.

[57] Ibid., p. 320.
[58] *NRS*, p. 235.
[59] Ibid., pp. 229–40.

In the meantime, the church in Germany was experiencing its own moments of enlightenment as to the true nature of what they had allowed to capture their souls.[60] The Pastors' Emergency League was not as effective dealing with the situation as some had hoped, leading to events that would culminate in the assembling of several church groups in Barmen and the beginnings of the Confessing Church. The centrepiece of this event would be the drafting of the Barmen Declaration, written by Karl Barth. In this document, the call was for those who would work to renounce the 'false doctrines' of the German Christian church government and confess the one true word of Jesus Christ.[61] While the Barmen Declaration was a strong call to resistance, it also failed to protest against the anti-Semitic racism of the time.

In this moment, Bonhoeffer found himself in a rather peculiar situation. Bethge reports that both the Confessing Church and the ecumenical movement, Bonhoeffer's only two communities of possible support, held him in suspicion. The Confessing Church was suspicious of Bonhoeffer's constant concern with the Sermon on the Mount, which they viewed as odd. The ecumenical movement was wary of his insistence on confession and the repudiation of heresy in the German church: 'He believed that the confessionally based opposition could be saved from sterility by the Sermon on the Mount, while that segment of the opposition with its roots in the Sermon on the Mount could be rescued from mere enthusiasm by the confession.'[62]

In the midst of all this, Hitler was tightening his hold on the hearts, minds and souls of the German people. Events were unfolding in Germany which were not advantageous to the strong resistance of opponents of the regime in either secular or ecclesiastical circles. Upon the death of Hindenburg, Hitler combined the two highest offices in Germany into his own person and was designated as *Führer*

---

[60] One such moment, the Sports Palace Demonstration of November 1933, put matters into bold relief for those who may have been deceived about the totalitarian and anti-Semitic claims of the Nazis. The language used by Dr Reinhard Krause, a leading party leader, in which he called for 'liberation from the Old Testament with its Jewish money morality and from these stories of cattle dealers and pimps.' particularly caught the attention of the press and those in the German Christian movement who preferred their anti-Semitism a little less vulgar.

[61] For the complete text of the Barmen Declaration in English translation, the reader can consult Arthur C. Cochrane's *The Church's Confession Under Hitler* (Philadelphia, PA: Westminster Press, 1962), pp. 237–42.

[62] Bethge, p. 372.

and Reich chancellor of the German people. Soon would follow oaths of allegiance to Hitler that would mean the loss of his position at Bonn for Karl Barth and an exile from Germany into Switzerland. Most Christians in Germany were overwhelmingly thrilled to have law and order reign. Hitler was, for them, their savior.

With this ferment as the backdrop, the ecumenical movement was preparing for an upcoming youth conference in Fanø, off the coast of Denmark, in August of 1934. Both sides of the church struggle expended no small effort to designate who should attend this conference as the official church representatives from Germany. The resolution of the issue would be profound, for the ecumenical council threw its weight on the side of the Confessing Church. This, of course, just caused more vitriol to be visited upon the ecumenical movement by those aligned with the German Christians.

Bonhoeffer was to deliver an address at Fanø that would draw much interest, even down to the present day. The document, entitled 'The Universal Church and the World of Nations', became known as Bonhoeffer's 'peace speech'. In a densely packed homily Bonhoeffer lays out the argument that peace on earth is a commandment given at Christ's coming. We can respond to this call by being obedient, or we can start the hypocritical questioning of the serpent in the garden, who asks, 'Has God really said . . .?' In powerful language, Bonhoeffer lays out the wisdom of the world in response to the command of God. He puts sentiments into the mouth of the forces that keep us from keeping the command of God: 'Must God not really have said that we should work for peace, of course, but also make ready tanks and poison gas for security?' Even more telling, the voice of the tempter, according to Bonhoeffer asks us, 'Did God say you should not protect your own people? Did God say you should leave your own a prey to the enemy?'[63]

Bonhoeffer goes on to contend that the church transgresses the boundaries that are set for it in nation or race, it is a universal church with members throughout all peoples. Peace will not come from the political order because peace means giving yourself to God and the political order does not behave in this fashion. Peace does not come from individual witness, or even individual churches, rather peace comes from the ecumenical church of Christ, which offers a place

---

[63] This speech can be found in *NRS*, pp. 289–92. It is remarkable how much can be said in such a short period of time.

upon which to confront the claims and universal pretensions of the political realm. The political order is choked with its weapons and mistrust of others, this realm is unable to respond to the call of God, but the worldwide church of God can respond to the command of God by not taking up weapons against one another, because to do so is to take up weapons against Christ himself.[64]

As this conference ended, Bonhoeffer made his way back to London, but the ensuing events in Germany were following the usual course. The Confessing Church continued to struggle not only with the Reich church, but with elements within its own ranks that sought compromise with the Nazis in order to ensure the survival of their church. Events would soon move to accent the necessity of beginning a seminary for training pastors from the Confessing Church movement, in no small part because candidates for theological examinations in the official state church had to prove they were of 'Aryan' descent.

Bonhoeffer was still in his parish in England, but the call came to him to consider taking on the responsibility of heading a new seminary for training the pastors nurtured by the Confessing Church. He accepted this invitation and began preparations for a trip to India, but this was not to be.[65] On 26 April 1934, Dietrich Bonhoeffer made his way to Zingst on the Baltic Sea where a new chapter would begin in his life and work.

[64] In an interesting sentence, Bonhoeffer mentions the people of the West being put to shame by non-Christians in the East. At this time, he had expressed an interest in going to visit Gandhi. The issue of Bonhoeffer's attraction to pacifism is not quite settled, because many see him as a pacifist given his statements about this in his speeches and writings, but others, most notably Bethge himself, argue that Bonhoeffer never was a pacifist. For now it is at least the case that it is immensely difficult being a solitary pacifist because this form of resistance is too difficult without the support and discipline of the community of Christ.

[65] This trip was to be undertaken in order that Bonhoeffer might join the ashram of his favourite prophet of the early 1930s, Mahatma Gandhi. Bonhoeffer's interest in India was actually long-standing and he had obtained permission to join Gandhi's ashram in a trip that was to take place in 1935. Bonhoeffer actually wrote Reinhold Niebuhr asking for his advice about this visit, and Niebuhr responded with opposition, in no small part because he believed that Gandhi was effective against the British because of their political liberalism. The Nazis, Niebuhr contended, would have no pangs of conscience about crushing resistance to their agendas. Rasmussen, *Dietrich Bonhoeffer: Reality and Resistance*, pp. 213–17.

A COSTLY GRACE

It was the work with the students of the new seminary that would partially mark Bonhoeffer's impact on the Christian church, especially
through his two writings from this period, *Discipleship* and *Life Together.*
The students under Bonhoeffer's charge soon moved from Zingst to
Finkenwalde where they would study, worship and prepare for life in
the church. Ironically, many of them would end up serving the needs
of the Nazi war machine and several would lose their lives to Hitler's
ambitions. The state for its part had not left its pretensions for control
of events alone and abandoned, and so maneuvered things legally that
the Confessing Church soon fell apart because of irreparable schisms.[66]
This would also impact the seminary at Finkenwalde as the Gestapo
would come to close it.

The days at Finkenwalde began and ended with worship, and the
discipline of the community was developed as they went along. They
lived in close quarters and so were together more intensely than would
have been the case at a university. Even so, the students were not themselves radicals and many were ready to serve the German government
through the military. This desire arose from the cultural conditioning
occasioned by life in Germany, but the desire to serve the government
also emerged because many in the Confessing Church wanted to show
that they were, at heart, a patriotic and loyal citizenry. There was no
real embrace of pacifism among the students even though their theological leader may have over the course of several evenings raised the
question for discussion.[67]

The experiment at Finkenwalde attracted its own share of notoriety
and visits from interested parties, but the students continued on in
their preparations. The usual subjects were taught: church history,
liturgics, pastoral care, biblical exegesis and the like, but there was
one novel aspect of this community and that was Bonhoeffer's own
lectures on discipleship. This was reflective of the centre of everything
that took place there and would be the heart and soul of how the

---

[66] This was done mostly through an act that appeared in September of 1935, the
Law for the Protection of the German Evangelical Church. This law effectively brought the
church totally under state control which made active resistance to the government itself
difficult for those raised to accept the tenets of Romans 13 that government is given by
God for good. Bethge, p. 421.

[67] Bethge, p. 431.

community formed. Though the theological training was rigorous and fully academic, there was still Bonhoeffer's unique desire to offer serious reflection on how the life of faith is lived in concrete ways. In some ways the concerns that were academic for him in the ecclesiology he explored in *Sanctorum Communio* now had become living reality. How does the church that incarnates Jesus Christ take concrete form in the world?

Bonhoeffer realized that with the events taking place around him theology must be done very carefully and with full discernment. Theology would be important for the role it played in legitimating certain positions of the German Christians. One such idea on the theological agenda was the doctrine of creation, or more specifically, in what way do the orders of society reflect God's ordering of human existence? Under this rubric a number of theological perspectives were being brought forth that essentially argued for the inherent sanctity of the state as 'order of creation'. Given the designs of Hitler, however, this type of theology just became justification for an idolatry of power, the baptizing of the state and its agenda with a Christian veneer.[68]

In these concerns, Bonhoeffer was still struggling with a theme that had challenged him for quite some time – how does the Sermon on the Mount inform the disciple of Christ? What is one to make of its revolutionary demands to extend grace in ways that seem impossible to maintain in the world? In what way does grace become costly as opposed to 'cheap'? Bonhoeffer wrote his lectures on discipleship in the midst of daily life within this community and it would be the last time in his life he would be surrounded by an ecclesial community that could nourish and stimulate his thinking about the distinct form that Christianity must take in order to respond to the world. This world

---

[68] Bethge writes concerning this: 'To show any interest, however genuine and earnest, in this particular subject at this particular time would come dangerously close to making an offer on the altar of Hitler.' Ibid., p. 459. Hence theologies of order would have to be met with theologies of breakthrough, which in some ways is what Bonhoeffer was working through at Finkenwalde. This was not done to isolate the church or constitute withdrawal of the church from the world; on the contrary, Bonhoeffer understood that the world needed something new:

> *Discipleship* is a call to battle, it is concentration and hence restriction, so that the entire earth may be reconquered by the infinite message . . . when the penultimate in its lust for glory and its thirst for adulation and sacrifice, thrust itself forward – and even in the church those who bowed before them were legion – Bonhoeffer turned towards the ultimate, for the sake of penultimate.

would soon become one in which his colleagues and students would be arrested in growing numbers.

The themes that emerged in *Discipleship* were oriented to Bonhoeffer's struggle for an authentic expression of Christ's church on earth. One aspect of this struggle was that the emphasis in the Christian faith is definitely not on the individual *qua* individual, but on the person as they exist within the community of faith. Although the individual does not disappear, they are still to be formed by the graces present within the community through its worship and life. This call to the community of Christ was done in recognition that all life is lived in the realm of the real and thus the community of faith would have to have a certain provisional and *ad hoc* quality about it.

There was a certain intensity in the particular community at Finkenwalde that led to searches for ways that the faithful might find expression for the teaching they were receiving. One such expression was the creation of a 'house of the brethren' in the preachers' seminary. This would be a community of persons committed to a more rigorous life than the seminary at large, a life together.[69] This community would incorporate the disciplines of confession, prayer, the care of souls, and other aspects of Christian formation that would mark a new way of being in the world. The first community was formed in September of 1935, consisting of six students who stayed behind in Finkenwalde while the other seminarians took vacations or breaks. This community would exist at Finkenwalde until the Gestapo closed the seminary itself in the autumn of 1937.[70]

This action on the part of the Gestapo actually hastened the appearance of the book *Life Together*, for Bonhoeffer was reluctant to publicize the experiment in community too soon. In Protestant Germany, this seemed far too Catholic, too exotic. In truth, however, Finkenwalde and its common life had revealed that the Protestant faith had

---

[69] It is interesting to think about this in relationship to Luther's exploration of this in his notion of *ecclesiolae in ecclesium*, the small church within the church. The idea of the church within the church attracted him as well, but upon further reflection Luther could not actually carry through on this because of his theology of *simul justus et peccator*, that we are simultaneously justified and sinner. This provided Luther with the realization that since we are simultaneously justified and sinner we cannot make claim to the type of purity that the committed community engendered by its very presence.

[70] Bethge himself was one of the initial members of this community. Bethge, p. 468.

suffered a type of impoverishment of spiritual formation that neglect of the larger Christian tradition offers. The larger tradition contained the resources that could lead to one's allowing oneself to be formed by adherence to disciplines that change one's orientation to life in the world. This constitutes one of the most enduring legacies of Bonhoeffer as we shall later see.

As always in Bonhoeffer's life, matters outside of Finkenwalde were proceeding as the regime dictated. Hitler in September of 1935 had announced the Nuremberg Laws, which were another phase of Jewish persecution. This was to be expected from Hitler, but more distressing was the report from Franz Hildebrandt to Bonhoeffer that the Confessing synod that was meeting was considering approving the Nuremberg Laws through conceding the state's right to legislate all questions concerning the Jews. The very fact that these were on the table stands as an embarrassment for the Confessing Church, but their tepid response signalled even bigger problems to come. Not the least of these were the attempts of the church to derive its legitimacy through its legal status and not its legal status through its legitimacy.[71]

The schools that were started outside the usual state institutions, such as Finkenwalde, were always suspect by those who remained within the official church's orbit. Ludwig Müller had already declared Finkenwalde illegal. But a ratcheting up of pressure was to be applied by laws passed by the Nazi bureaucracy that also declared such schools to be illegal in the eyes of the state. This made it pretty much impossible for students who were preparing for parish work to find positions in the church. Those who came to Finkenwalde did so in the realization that they were paying a price by attending.[72] For some that price was too dear and so they departed to attend schools that were approved

---

[71] Shelley Baranowski covers part of this story in her contribution to the afore-mentioned book, *Betrayal.* Her chapter, entitled, 'The Confessing Church and Anti-semitism: Protestant Identity, German Nationhood, and the Exclusion of the Jews' portrays many of the difficulties and ambiguities that marked the Confessing church, pp. 90–109.

[72] For example, the passage of the Fifth Implementation Decree which was the means whereby the state assumed absolute power over the church was devastating in its implications and showed what the church was up against. Bethge, pp. 496–97. Another manifestation of this price can be seen in Bishop Heckel's statement to the Prussian church committee calling Bonhoeffer an enemy of the state and even worse, a pacifist. For these crimes, he should not be allowed to train German theologians. In this condemnation of Bonhoeffer's purported pacifism, Heckel stood in common with almost all Christians in Germany, even those of Finkenwalde. Bethge, pp. 511–12.

by the state church. This took its toll on the rest of the community and especially Bonhoeffer. These conflicts only mirrored the internal erosion that was taking place in the Confessing church as the pressures being exerted within and without caused their own fissures.

For Bonhoeffer, matters came to a head when he returned from an unauthorized (by the state) visit to Sweden, which created quite the stir in Germany. His right to teach at the University of Berlin was revoked. But this was merely one in a series of actions the state was taking against those who had put themselves in resistance to the official church organization. Life at Finkenwalde continued despite these disruptions and the students not only continued in their studies, but in their sense of mission as well.

As 1936 drew to a close, changes were occurring that would turn out ominous for the community. The Gestapo continued its work of harassing and arresting people who it deemed enemies of the state and this included pastors. By the end of 1937, 804 members of the Confessing Church had been imprisoned for various durations.[73] In effect this took place through the means of onerous regulations meant to squeeze those elements of the church that still organized outside of state purview. Communications between parties were made impossible and even collections were forbidden during Confessing Church services. On July 1, the Gestapo would arrest Martin Niemöller, a leader in the Confessing Church. Bonhoeffer became involved with this because he was visiting Niemöller later that day unaware that he had been arrested. He encountered the Gestapo at the house where he was questioned and detained.

Events escalated as the authorities stepped up the arrests and the repression as former Finkenwaldians were arrested and removed from their positions. It was only a matter of time before the final blow, which came in September when the Gestapo showed up in Finkenwalde with orders to shut it down. Similar scenes were playing out all over Germany and the light of these schools grew dimmer and dimmer, finally to be extinguished.

On a Long Distant Shore

For most of the years between 1938 and 1941, Bonhoeffer lived in the rather remote reaches of outer Pomerania where he sought to sustain

---

[73] Ibid., p. 577.

pastoral leadership and remain in the fight. This was discouraging because he watched with disappointment as the Confessing Church continued to be more concerned with its own survival than the larger picture of what was taking place among the nations. Among the most heartbreaking moments must have been when Bonhoeffer heard that over 85 per cent of Confessing Church pastors had signed the oath of loyalty to Hitler in 1938. This only contributed to Bonhoeffer's sense of isolation, as the community that he had placed great hope in became dissipated by the Nazi machinery. Even worse, many took the loyalty oath knowing that there was an impending order that non-Aryans must have a large 'J' stamped on their identity cards.[74]

But this was becoming business as usual for a country that had slipped under the totalitarian thumb of the National Socialists. The types of repression that took place in Germany led to a situation where people who were active, who might have wanted to know what was going on, soon found that life goes easier if one ignores the construction taking place behind the trees, outside the village. A psychology of repression serves as a dark cloud that descends upon a people, and the questions formerly asked no longer find willing expression. It was this that Bonhoeffer faced and the church could not provide a community strong enough to meet this challenge. He would find people who would take up the challenge of his time, but they would not do so because of commitment to Christ.

One such person was Hans von Dohnanyi, his brother-in-law, who was working with others in the military and the political order to form some type of resistance within Germany. It was to this circle that von Dohnanyi introduced Bonhoeffer. Some of these were persons in the military intelligence which is where Bonhoeffer would eventually find himself. It is within this circle that Bonhoeffer learned more than he previously knew about the political situation within the Reich. Meantime, events orchestrated by Hitler were, from his perspective, going extremely well, including the march into Austria in March of 1938. After this, it became obvious that former measures to try and blunt Hitler were not going to have an effect. The resistance must be a military one, which itself was difficult because Hitler was skillful at turning the levers of power of state in an ever more suffocating way around his desires and oversight.

As the country went on war footing, Bonhoeffer found himself subject to call up in the military, but before that could take place he found

---

[74] Ibid., p. 603.

himself in a familiar place, Union Theological Seminary in New York City. He had been considering a visit to America during his time in London during March and April of 1939. As events unfolded, he landed in America in June of 1939 and was immediately beset by inner doubts about the course of action he had taken. It was an excruciating time for him. In a famous letter to Reinhold Niebuhr, he wrote:

> I have come to the conclusion that I have made a mistake in coming to America. I must live through this difficult period of our national history with the Christian people of Germany. I will have no right to participate in the reconstruction of Christian life in Germany after the war if I do not share the trials of this time with my people . . . Christians in Germany will face the terrible alternative of either willing the defeat of their nation in order that Christian civilization may survive, or willing the victory of their nation and thereby destroying our civilization.[75]

On 7 July, he was on a boat as it made its way out of New York to head back to Germany and the last stage of Bonhoeffer's life. His brother, Karl-Friedrich, was returning to Germany from America as well.

Now Bonhoeffer was to enter a new phase of his life, marked by his more active, though still peripheral work with the *Abwehr*, the military intelligence wing that housed several of the conspirators against the regime. This was not an immediate consideration upon his return to Germany, but would slowly come into focus for Bonhoeffer as the succeeding months unfolded. At first he went back to his collective parish work, overseeing his former students in the countryside of Germany, and writing. Though he had several places around Germany where he worked, he really had no settled home other than his parents' house in Berlin. Hitler was wildly successful during this time with France being the big victory that solidified his power and made opposition to him that much more difficult.

Under these conditions, Bonhoeffer kept as much contact as he could with former students and others in the Confessing Church movement. These contacts were difficult due to restrictions of the regime and also because so many former students were scattered over the war zones. The collective pastorates of his former students were dissolved in March of 1940 and Bonhoeffer found himself without a job. It did not help that later that year he would be forbidden to speak in public

---

[75] See *A Testament to Freedom: The Essential Writings of Dietrich Bonhoeffer*, revised edition. Edited by Geffrey B. Kelly and F. Burton Nelson (New York, NY: HarperCollins, 1995), p. 504.

on the grounds that this would constitute 'subversive activity'.[76] Along with this prohibition came the order to report regularly on his movements to the police.

Bonhoeffer fought these restrictions, but to little relief. In the meantime, he continued his work on what would come to constitute *Ethics*. His other choice at this time was to join the conspirators more closely by taking a position with military intelligence. This put Bonhoeffer in a particularly isolated position because many of his colleagues in the church and the ecumenical movement had no idea what to do with this information. To all outside eyes, it looked like Bonhoeffer had betrayed his deepest beliefs. There was a great deal of suspicion, especially about his motives in all this. This created no small agony for him.[77]

It was in these circumstances that Bonhoeffer was able to steal some time to work on the ethics material at Ettal monastery in the south of Germany. He had periods of uninterrupted time here to work, but surely all the events in his life were deeply on his mind as he sought to fashion *Ethics*. It should not go unnoticed that his work on this text was done basically alone and not within the community that formed the background for *Discipleship*.

The letters that he was reading from Finkenwaldians must have been heartbreaking as well, some of which reflected the ways in which war causes one to lose almost all morality, save the morality of the tribe.[78] By the end of the war over 75 former students at Finkenwalde would have lost their lives to this war. The needless destruction of this war was being felt by Bonhoeffer more deeply every day. For a theologian who was so concerned about the real and the concrete, this reality was a suffering all of its own.

This reality was the arena in which Bonhoeffer had to serve the rest of his life. After the fall of France in June of 1940 Hitler, like

[76] Bethge, p. 698. At this point in anticipation of what I want to raise later it must be observed that perhaps every Christian voice should be in danger of being silenced because it is subversive to business as usual and the way that society is being arranged by the powerful elites.

[77] Paradigmatic of this suspicion is surely the attitude of Karl Barth to this turn of events. Barth himself thought that Bonhoeffer must have finally given in and gone to the other side of the struggle. It was only with great effort that Bonhoeffer was able to convince Barth otherwise.

[78] Ibid., p. 704.

Napoleon, turned his attention to Russia. This would not begin officially until June of 1941. Bonhoeffer in the meantime entered into full service of the resisters by taking his first trip to Switzerland to meet with ecumenical leaders to apprise them of the situation in Germany. He also was able to meet with Karl Barth and tell him the truth about what he was up to with his new work. Other trips would follow, all with the intention of relating to the outside world what the situation in Germany looked like from the resister's point of view. Bonhoeffer and his contacts in church circles became useful to the resistance because he could help gauge how other Europe would respond when Hitler was overthrown. These efforts in some senses were helpful for explanations, but in other ways they were tragic defeats, especially regarding Bonhoeffer's mission to the British, through his contacts with Bell.[79]

In Germany in 1943 matters were coming to a head and events were rapidly moving. Hitler had overextended his army, which would sow the seeds of Germany's ultimate defeat and the conspirators felt it was time to move. The various intrigues among bureaucratic offices meant that the Gestapo was increasingly suspicious of what von Dohnanyi and others in the *Abwehr* were up to. There were two attempts on Hitler's life in March of 1943 that failed and, on 5 April 1943 the Gestapo came to Bonhoeffer's house in Berlin and arrested him. He was taken to the Tegel military interrogation prison. He was not the only one taken that day, as von Dohnanyi and his wife were also among those arrested.

From this point Bonhoeffer would be held a prisoner in Tegel and was to pen the fragments that made their way into the consciousness of the world under the title *Letters and Papers from Prison*. The words he wrote would find an audience who would interpret those words in various ways. We will have occasion to consider the reception of Bonhoeffer and his call for what a religionless Christianity might look like, but he reminds us that the lives we live are hidden in some ways that we cannot discern, even as we live in the midst of them.

His time in Tegel would be spent writing fiction, letters and theological reflections to his friends and family. As the war continued,

---

[79] The account of this is found in Bethge, pp. 757–75. This mission was undertaken on behalf of the resistance within the state that Bonhoeffer found himself within. Essentially those in places of political power were putting out feelers to the British government about what would happen to Germany if Hitler were overthrown. While Bell trusted Bonhoeffer, he was opposed by others in England who did not share Bell's view of what to do with Germany at the end of hostilities.

Bonhoeffer would experience great difficulties in his captivity, but his fate was sealed when Claus von Stauffenberg's attempt to assassinate Hitler failed on 20 July 1944. Two months later, evidence would be uncovered that linked Bonhoeffer to various members of the conspiracy and other members of his family would be arrested: Klaus, his brother and Rüdiger Schleicher, his brother-in-law. In October of that year, Bonhoeffer was transferred to the Gestapo prison at Prinz-Albrecht-Strasse, Berlin. This would start a series of moves that would culminate in Bonhoeffer being executed on 9 April 1945 at Flossenbürg with other key members of the conspiracy. On 30 April, Hitler would commit suicide in his bunker.

In a letter dated 23 February 1944, Bonhoeffer was reflecting on the ways our lives are shaped by all those forces that construct us and he wrote to Bethge that, 'The important thing today is that we should be able to discern for the fragment of our life how the whole was arranged and planned, and what material it consists of. For really there are some fragments that are only worth throwing into the dustbin . . . and others whose importance lasts for centuries, because their completion can only be a matter for God, and so they are fragments that must be fragments.'[80]

As we live among the fragments ourselves, we cannot know with certainty which ones will last. It becomes our task, even within our fractured world, to respond to our times. But, even so, we can certainly recognize that Bonhoeffer, for all his faults and weaknesses, constitutes a claim on us that is still compelling in these difficult times. In reflection on Bonhoeffer's struggles, we may find which of those fragments that constitute our lives will last for centuries.

---

[80] *LPP*, p. 219. My first impression to use the notion of fragments in regards to Bonhoeffer's life came from Stanley Hauerwas in *Performing the Faith: Bonhoeffer and the Practice of Nonviolence*, (Grand Rapids, Mich.: Brazos Press, 2004), p. 33.

Chapter 3

LIVING IN THE WORLD COME OF AGE

There is a scene in the movie *Schindler's List* that opens the film. The scene shows tables being set up on a railway platform, pens and paper being arranged so carefully as to suggest an overwhelming attention to order and propriety. Everything is in precise form, clean, neat and orderly. And then the trains come. As the human cargo spills out of the trains, we are confronted with the fact that all this efficiency has been put in the service of one of humanity's most soulless moments, the Holocaust. It serves as a compelling example of what Bonhoeffer called the 'world come of age' for the way that bureaucracy and technique functioned in the Nazi regime points to something significant for our day.

In this chapter, I wish to sketch out the contours of what Bonhoeffer was exploring in his captivity when he was reflecting on the metaphor of the 'world come of age'. I will trace out his thoughts on how the world developed intellectually and explore some of the ideas that emerged from his reflections in prison. In the second part, I want to point to places where I see Bonhoeffer's concept of a 'world come of age' having a significant impact on our time. By reflecting on the political and economic orders as they impact the West presently, I hope to lay out a marker for thinking through how faith responds to the 'world come of age' in the rest of the book.

Dietrich Bonhoeffer in his prison writings put forth the idea that humankind is living increasingly in a 'world come of age'. By this Bonhoeffer had in mind a world of increasing maturity that was able to arrange itself very well without the tutelage of religion or God. This maturation had actually been a theme in Bonhoeffer's writings since

1931–1932.[81] In these earlier writings, though, one can sense that the maturation of the world is not to be seen in an entirely positive light. The autonomy of humankind is not seen in a beneficial way.[82]

In the prison, letters we find new concepts and reflections entering his thought about the ways in which the development of humankind has led it to a 'world come of age'. The world that he is interpreting from within prison appears to him as autonomous in the sense of being freed from previous authorities that informed human consciousness. Now the life of humans appears to be lived from a deep sense of self-determination.

Beginning early in 1944 Bonhoeffer traces the growing autonomy of humankind back to the 13th century as he analyses the historical progression of human society in the West. In these letters, he lays out the contours of the 'world come of age', a world that is able to arrange its own affairs nicely, without God or any other authority who claims to speak for God interfering in humankind's freedom. In doing this he is very influenced by his reading of a number of different authors, among whom were Wilhelm Dilthey, José Ortega y Gasset and Carl Friedrich von Weizsäcker. In his reading of these people, Bonhoeffer is not so much concerned with theology as he is with probing the question of what the world really looks like, or what it has become.

No doubt this is in part because of the historical circumstances of his involvement with the conspiracy and the collapse of the church. He had plunged headlong into the life of political intrigue and actions against the government of Germany in some measure due to the collapse of the church. As he tackles the intellectual shaping and history of the world, his curiosity is piqued by how others have interpreted the world. What does the world look like from the perspective of those whom Bonhoeffer is reading?

In a letter dated 16 July 1944, Bonhoeffer traces this journey through a host of sources: Lord Herbert of Cherbury is mentioned as being one of the first who maintained that reason is sufficient for religious knowledge, in ethics the shift was made from divine commandments to humanly constructed rules for life, in politics Machiavelli detaches politics from morality and appeals to doctrine, replacing them with the authority of 'reasons of state', and Hugo Grotius sets up natural law as international law, which is valid *etsi deus non daretur* ('as though God does not exist', a phrase that would come to define Bonhoeffer). In philosophy the shift towards the world's maturation would continue

[81] See, for example, Wüstenberg, pp. 90–91.
[82] *DBW*, 10: 357–78.

with the work of Descartes, Spinoza and Kant. In natural law Nicholas of Cusa and Giordano Bruno would hypothesize an infinite universe that was self-subsisting, also *etsi deus non daretur.*[83]

Of prime importance to his thinking through this journey towards human autonomy was his reading of Wilhelm Dilthey's works, most notably his *Weltanschauung und Analyse des Menschen seit Renaissance und Reformation* (*Worldview and Analysis of Humans Since the Renaissance and Reformation*).[84] In this book Bonhoeffer read how the Enlightenment had created a different type of person, one whose independence could be found outside the confines of the past constructions of religion or morality. Dilthey described a history where a medieval metaphysics of God and the human had dissolved, to be replaced by human moral and intellectual autonomy. As this autonomy grew it became far more rooted in attention to this world's affairs rather than the concerns of the next world. Reason and rationality would serve as the guides to interpret human existence. But Dilthey himself was not interested in the notion of a disembodied, sterile rationality. He explored the embodied, living aspects of historical development and the way they impact the construction of human life.[85] It was this embodiment that especially attracted Bonhoeffer.

Dilthey believed that the natural and human sciences were able to offer us a particular and distinct perspective on existence that afforded humankind the ability to achieve the status of a neutral observer.

[83] This letter comes after other letters from Bonhoeffer's reading of Wilhelm Dilthey and others. This particular listing shows that he was consolidating his reading and thinking to form some core ideas of what a world come of age looked like.

[84] This was not the only book of Dilthey's that Bonhoeffer read and remarked on. In these other volumes, *Von deutscher Dichtung und Musik* (*German Poetry and Music*), and *Das Erlebnis und die Dichtung* (*Poetry and Experience*) Bonhoeffer was thinking about the role of the Enlightenment in shaping human existence and its reflective understanding. For the reader who is interested in learning more about the way that Dilthey developed his ideas of *Weltanschauung* there are English translations of Dilthey's works published by Princeton University Press under the editorship of Rudolf A. Makkreel and Frithjof Rodi. Dilthey was important to Bonhoeffer at this juncture in providing him a way of interpreting history. Dilthey's understanding of the role of the sciences would have a profound impact on Bonhoeffer's understanding of the 'natural'. This was not Bonhoeffer's first exposure to Dilthey, however, as he remarks on his hermeneutical theory earlier.

[85] Some of the most extensive treatments of Dilthey's influence on Bonhoeffer can be found in Wüstenberg, pp. 104–12; 136–47. Another Bonhoeffer scholar who deals with this is Ernst Feil, *The Theology of Dietrich Bonhoeffer*, trans. Martin Rumscheidt (Philadelphia, PA: Fortress Press, 1985). Of course, Dilthey had a profound impact on how the western world interpreted itself with his work in hermeneutics, social theory and the sciences.

He believed in a certain approach to the human sciences that would complement the natural sciences in order to better understand the 'natural' world. This grasping of what was 'natural' would result in knowing the world in such a way that one could divine what principles, structures, norms, concepts and laws guided the world and its history. In this way, humankind could achieve freedom from nature itself. In art, politics, morality, ethics and science we learn through both the human and natural sciences how to construct and live in the world in a freedom not available to humankind previous to the 'world come of age'.

Thus the emergence of natural science resulted in a particular way of understanding the world that involved the discovery of 'facts' about the world by the methods it had developed. These facts, though, were still isolated from a larger narrative that would offer a pattern to what were random aspects of nature in such a way as to provide coherence and a grasp of reality. Dilthey believed that what he called the human sciences could help fill this gap. The human sciences like hermeneutics, for example, were an effective means of constructing worldviews out of physical reality.

On 8 June, 1944 Bonhoeffer wrote about this world:

> The movement that began about the thirteenth century . . . towards the autonomy of man (in which I should include the discovery of laws by which the world lives and deals with itself in science, social and political matters, art, ethics, and religion) has in our time reached an undoubted completion. Man has learnt to deal with himself in all questions of importance without recourse to the 'working hypothesis' called 'God'.[86]

Bonhoeffer understood that the consciousness of the world was changed, and from his cell he believed that humankind would, through its sciences, find the keys for a reading of laws that guided the world: 'The world that has become conscious of itself and the laws which govern its own existence has grown self-confident in what seems to us to be an uncanny way.'[87]

In exploring the ways in which consciousness is formed and social arrangements legitimated, Bonhoeffer comes to see that the world makes these arrangements very well without resorting to God:

> God as a working hypothesis in morals, politics or science, has been surmounted and abolished; and the same thing has happened in philosophy and religion

---

[86] *LPP*, 325.
[87] Ibid., 326.

(Feuerbach!). For the sake of intellectual honesty, that working hypothesis should be dropped, or as far as possible eliminated. A scientist or physician who sets out to edify is a hybrid.[88]

In the 'world come of age' religion no longer dominates the social structures that shape the world. Reflecting on the world since the Reformation Bonhoeffer, whose life and work had existed in the strong connection between the Lutheran expression of the state church and all the connections to culture that went with that, saw some things differently than before. Now the organic connection between throne and altar that had defined the Christian religion for centuries seemed to no longer make any sense. And yet one paradox in this is that Bonhoeffer saw the state as a necessary element in maintaining order by the restraint of evil. Even in the *Ethics* Bonhoeffer does not seem to want to jettison this tie between the state and the Christian religion.[89]

This connection between religion and the social order, though, predated the appearance of the Christian religion and has been found in many ancient societies. The process of secularization that Bonhoeffer reflected upon can be traced back as far as Israel's construction of its religious ethos in relationship to the cultures it found itself within.[90] This led ancient Israel's theologians to a certain rationalization about

[88] Ibid., 360.

[89] This can be a little difficult with Bonhoeffer since he uses different terms at different times to try and work out how the church and state relate to one another. Rejecting the idea that there is an inherent connection between the two as one might find in the 'orders of creation' theology, he argued for an order of preservation to try and counter the ideas found in the idea of the 'orders of creation'. Later in his life he addressed this issue through the use of language that spoke of 'mandates'. This is found in other places, but significantly makes its appearance in the writings that comprise *Ethics* in several sections. For our purposes, the main issue is that Bonhoeffer wanted to detach historical and contingent forms of government from being inherently seen as an expression of God's will. See *Ethics*, pp. 68–75; 388–94.

[90] See, for example, Berger when he gives his analysis of how Israel defined itself over against cultures that had embedded the Divine within the processes of nature, leading to practices that must be kept in order to maintain a certain sense of cosmic order. Israel responds to this by locating Elohim, the God above all gods, outside the cosmos in a transcendence that issues in ethical demands, but not a sacralization of nature itself. There is a sense in which Israel demythologizes the world around it by a certain rationalization of law and contractual and conventional tradition. Peter Berger, *The Sacred Canopy: Elements of a Sociological Theory of Religion* (New York, NY: Anchor Books), 1990. For the reader interested in pursuing these themes, I would suggest that they look at Charles Taylor's *A Secular Age* (Cambridge, MA: Belknap Press, 2007).

the world that vacated it in some senses of the presence of spiritual forces.[91] Throughout the prison correspondence though, Bonhoeffer sees this notion of this-worldliness as an aspect of Jewish life that is necessary for Christians to recover.[92]

In this process of maturation, the world was developing a new consciousness and a new sense of the self was also being created. This self was no longer located in those institutions, such as the church, which had previously defined it, but now was to be found within a host of secular and cultural influences. The suspicion of powers such as the church that modernity had engendered had led the modern world to trust in the self-authenticating power of critical reason and rigorous rationality. The new world would be constructed on the way that we, not God, would interpret life, whether through law, morality, religion or the sciences.

SCIENCE, A NEW AUTHORITY

Bonhoeffer understood that this historical movement constituted a new authority that had replaced religion in the construction of the 'world come of age' and he was particularly interested in learning more about science. In a letter dated 2 February 1944, Bonhoeffer says that he needs a working knowledge of Dilthey and that it was a great regret to him that he was so ignorant of the natural sciences. He followed up this regret by finding a book by C. F. von Weizsäcker, *Worldview of Physics*, from which he hoped to learn a great deal.[93] It is obvious that he had read it right after receiving it, judging from his comment on 29 May that the book was keeping him busy thinking about the way that science had impacted humankind's coming of age.[94]

As later writings would show, Bonhoeffer was very much influenced by the understanding that science is able to answer an increasingly

[91] Think, for example, of the way in which the first creation account in Genesis appears to finds its origin during Israel's captivity in Babylon. The Jewish account is decidedly different from the Enuma Elish and its orders of violence and mythologies.

[92] See, for example, Bonhoeffer's letter of 27 June when he writes about how Israel defines the notion of redemption as being historical, on this side of death. It is this world and living before God in it that is the crucial piece. *LPP*, 336.

[93] Ibid., p. 308.

[94] In a comment made in the 16 July 1944 letter, Bonhoeffer remarks on physics and the infinite universe in such a way as to indicate that he was taking some ideas from the reading from Weizsäcker, pp. 359–60.

number of questions that previously religion had maintained a monopoly on. Inasmuch as science was a part of humankind's putting away an immature view of the world, it did perform an absolutely necessary service. Its interpretations of the world were not only useful, but could be proven by testable hypothesis and public examination of the data. Here was no appeal to the person's inner revelation of God, but a means whereby truth could be understood and accepted on mutually agreed terms. No wonder this was such a turning point in the creation of the modern world.

The role of the sciences not only to examine the natural world, but to interpret and narrate the world the way that those who accepted the assumptions of modernity believed, has been a strong shaper of our understanding. Today the natural and human sciences stand as the pre-eminent authority of the secular order to determine what home looks like to the citizens of its domain. Bonhoeffer contended that theological attempts to resist this authority have been relatively useless.[95]

Yet in his treatment of Dilthey's understanding of the 'natural' Bonhoeffer does not see the power of science to narrate to us exactly what nature looks like. Science offers the power to interpret nature in a particular way because it offers epistemologies of control. The natural sciences can control how we think about nature and the world every bit as much as religion can. It functions as an instrument of control because it establishes meaning and purpose for many who have no use for the hypothesis of God.

Meaning and purpose in the scientific model are to be decided on the basis of material and efficient causalities. In other words, all understanding about the world is provided by explanations of events that are found within matter. Comets are not signs of God's judgement, leading to the building of a cathedral; they are natural occurrences, explainable by natural laws. When life is explained along these lines, it creates a notion of causality that will establish for humankind the final rationalities in which it becomes embedded.

For example, our captivity to our creations in some ways creates us because we become what we make and every artefact we create on the basis of our technologies in turn creates us. The more embedded we become in these technologies, for example, computers, the less able we become to be reflective about their impact on us. In an odd turn,

[95] See, for example, his comments on this in the 30 June 1944 letter, p. 341.

the more autonomous we think we become, the more captivated by our creations we become.

This is partially one of the powers that science possesses; it vacates the world of any other worth or meaning save what is embedded in nature. The hidden assumption in all this is that we are interpreting nature accurately enough to reflect what is truly there. A particular type of science that sees itself as possessing ultimate power to interpret nature means that the pretension to control engendered by the Enlightenment remains intact. One of the great problems about this is that it can narrow our ability to think or imagine what nature actually looks like.

In Bonhoeffer's understanding, gained from his reading of Weizsäcker, he sees science as continually moving the frontiers and boundaries of human knowledge. This is an inevitable process and necessary for the maturation of the world. Through his reading of Dilthey he welcomed the dissipation of medieval metaphysics, but the totality of what this means is that as the world comes to its own sense of autonomy, it will substitute its own causalities to interpret the world, resulting in a type of secular teleology, where the ends are pre-determined by the means.

Bonhoeffer saw that the shared communal assumptions of improving material life and the value of rigorous reasoning and empirical verification can lead us to a better life in this world. We do not need recourse to God when nature destroys our homes; we have insurance. However, we also pay a cost for these things in the 'world come of age'. We give ourselves over to rationalities that dictate how life in the world is lived. All meaning becomes collapsed into that which is scientifically explainable and 'rational'. Resistance to the orders created in this world becomes 'irrational' and futile.

What was new in this was that Bonhoeffer no longer saw this movement towards human autonomy in a purely negative light. The process of secularization could lead to positive results in some ways because the useless aspects of life could be sliced away to reveal our true standing in the world. Bethge comments on this:

> Secularization was no longer an evil falling away, but the free responsibility of Christianity; the secularizers were no longer powerful seducers, but the protagonists and midwives of humanity. The issue is recognizing a development that eventually will make the church guilty if it continues to demonize worldliness, instead of helping human beings realize their true humanity.[96]

---

[96] Bethge, p. 869.

The new space created by these historical processes does not mean an unqualified acceptance of the new world, it means that things can be more honestly understood than before. And in this honesty, both the positive and the negative can be faced with a new type of discernment.

When Bonhoeffer asks the question of what Christianity is for us, the 'us' aspect takes central focus. Who are we? What has the world's maturation brought to us to in our time? How is the world these days, and who are we in it? Bonhoeffer thought when clear-eyed examination was turned here we could discover all types of things as long as we did not try to hide behind the shields of denial or traditions that we had constructed.

Bonhoeffer was asking what animated his world. What were the forces that had propelled it to the place that he now occupied? His interpretation for this was provided by the entire context of his life, but in the prison correspondence he had the occasion to ask new questions about how reason and the confidence of humankind in its own abilities had led the world to come of age. In this way, Bonhoeffer serves as a guide for us as well, because he is asking the type of questions we also need to ask about the world that we are presently constructing.

WHAT IS THE WORLD FOR US?

So, this question remains for us as well. What does the 'world come of age' look like to us today? Where have we been led in the process that Bonhoeffer thinks about in 1944? The recognition that secularity and ironically, religion, had come to define his world offered Bonhoeffer an unsentimental view of matters. He accepted the reality that human history had shaped his context in such a way that it provided a social emancipation from previous authorities. But from within that autonomy politics, economics, morals and religion had all failed to adequately confront the realities of the moment in which he lived. This confluence of institutions was precisely where the world needed to be engaged, though Bonhoeffer did not believe that this engagement should be one where believers try and justify God before the world because that just replicated the mistake of using God to fill the world's gaps.

The trajectory that Bonhoeffer was following much of his life and is tracing in the letters of 1944 provided him a new self-awareness, a new consciousness about how the world had been formed, the dynamics of how we interpret the world, and the ways in which our interpretations become the new communally assumed realities. We will use our science, our reason, to build a world where we can exercise our full creative powers. This is not necessarily a thing to be mourned or resisted, though discernment of where the world was going and how to respond to it from Christian faith was crucial in accurately understanding life.

In the years since Bonhoeffer was writing in his cell we have become more aware than ever of the productive aspects of humanity upon the world. We are conscious that we shape the world even as we are shaped by it. Yet, many of the citizens of the 'world come of age' have not yet come to the realization that our deepest held communal assumptions about aspects of culture that shape our very identities are themselves historically and temporally conditioned.

In the 'world come of age' both the material (politics, economics, travel) and the non-material (race, gender, philosophy) aspects of our very lives are creations of our hands. We are the ones who assign a certain type of value to them. We are the ones who determine whether a certain order of existence is good or proper and then we invest enormous energies in protecting our constructions from alternatives. This works in politics, religion or economics, just to name a few places.

And this is the truth we are so resistant to in the modern world. We spend ample time telling ourselves that our narrations of the world are rooted in something solid, something transcendent, that which should not even be questioned. No matter who we are, or where we live, we are continually being asked to just accept that the roles/ideas/beliefs that shape us are 'just the way things are'. If you doubt the power of accepted assumptions, then raise questions about whether the political and social order you live under is legitimate and wait for the voices of indignation to arise.

The social world we create is taken for granted and dissent becomes unthinkable. To deny the accepted order of your society is to put yourself outside the realm of the community. You become a non-being, susceptible to disappearing in ways subtle and all too real. Cultural and historical location is a powerful force in how consciousness is formed and it is one of the things that Bonhoeffer was struggling with in the Tegel writings. I suspect that in some ways he intuited where his thoughts were taking him, though they did not come to full fruition because of a life cut short.

In the full autonomy of the 'world come of age' we are the creators of the world, and that which we create we also hold the illusion we control. It is a fiction, but one that modern humankind accommodates itself to with only slight discomfort. What we have created has been established by '. . . the institutional and cultural concomitants of economic growth under the conditions of sophisticated technology.'[97] The features of this are well known to us – the rise of the nation-state, science and technological establishments, capitalism and mass media among others. As mentioned at the start of this chapter the 'world come of age' concerns itself with technique and ultimately, through the technologies we have devised, control.

As we have seen, in the 'world come of age' the concept of rationality plays a large role. Science and the distinct rationality it generated would be the one place that an exhausted world could seemingly gather that would not be contested ground. After the Reformation the unity of Christian society in the West collapsed and with it a certain type of civil peace. The resulting miasma led to no small confusion about whose religion was to be privileged and thus worthy of being protected. But political factors were far more prevalent in the conflicts that arose after the Reformation than religion.

Given the resultant explosion of ideas conceived in human thought it seemed inevitable that religion, especially when it became a tool used by the political order to mobilize forces for its agendas, would cause no small mischief in the affairs of humankind. By the end of this process Europe was so fatigued and disgusted by the violence generated by political wars fueled by appeals to religious emotion, that the appeal to the authority of reason and rationality was met with acclaim.[98]

Humankind sought a universal ground of understanding to which everyone had access. Or, at least, everyone who accepted the assumptions

---

[97] Peter Berger, *Pyramids of Sacrifice: Political Ethics and Social Change* (Garden City, NY: Anchor, 1976), p. 34.

[98] William T. Cavanaugh has a perceptive take on the relationship between religion and the state, arguing essentially that the mythology of the wars of religion fought in the aftermath of the Reformation served the state's desire for taking power from religious institutions, and thus served as a narrative of control. The complex history that resulted from this has led exactly to the world come of age. '"A Fire Strong Enough to Consume the House": The Wars of Religion and the Rise of the State,' *Modern Theology* 11:4 (October 1995), pp. 397–420.

of what reason and rationality looked like to those at the time. The attraction of a commonly accepted rationality meant no one had to entertain seriously claims to revelation that were not publicly verifiable. And most assuredly social structures did not have to be built to conform to the revelations of the religious.

But what was not so apparent at the dawn of the Enlightenment was that a universally accepted rationality would itself prove to be elusive. Though the pretensions of the Enlightenment fully anticipated the day when reason would make everything so apparent all but mad persons could agree on what was rational, we have come instead to a place where we find that all structures of contemporary society operate under diverse concepts of rationality, the most dominant of which in the western world usually entails a certain ends/means calculus. Pragmatism has become the operative dynamic of many social structures.

When modern humanity thinks in terms of a 'rational' path of action the actors usually have some understanding of where following the rational path will lead. Being rational means the best way to reach this goal. The result of this type of thinking means a certain expectation is formed that everyone line up behind whatever rationality is regnant at any given time, because to do or think otherwise would be non-rational. This dynamic can constitute a type of secular teleology, where the ends prescribe the means to reach it.

The more integrated we become to the logics of modernity and its definitions of rationality the less able we are to recognize what another order of life would truly look like. In the 'world come of age' that we struggle with, our lives have been shaped by the inexorable logics that have come to dominate human existence with an absoluteness that rivals anything religion has ever been able to manage. This is why even rationality itself becomes defined in such a way that to question it makes the questioner suspect in the eyes of the supposedly rational. In this way rationality, as it has emerged and constructed the world we live in, exercises its own control and power to determine what is 'rational' or 'orderly'.

The Enlightenment project that Bonhoeffer was exploring with his prison reflections has itself hit hard times as the relentless critique of contemporary life has emerged with all its force. But, in the larger concerns of the world, the truth that we are the creators of rationalities that we embrace as self-evident truths has not yet become one of those assumptions most people consider when they reflect on the world and our place in it. The irony, of course, is that when we do come to a clear understanding of how this works it will be yet another step on the path that Bonhoeffer welcomed, the maturity of humankind. A greater recognition of historical contingency, fought by many, has the potential of offering humanity the great gift of humility, though it should be obvious why politicians will fight this awareness.

But, for the moment, let us take a look at how the 'world come of age' has fared since Bonhoeffer. As stated above, we construct the world around certain logics and rationalities we ourselves devise. These logics (and hence the rationalities) of modernity have been constructed around ideology (the state and all its attendant bureaucracies) and economics (for all intents and purposes the forms of capitalism that presently hold hegemony in the world). When Bonhoeffer probed 'the world come of age' he wrote under the shadow of a strongly totalitarian order that stood on the foundation of these forces.

The emancipation from previous social structures like the church formed the impetus for the creation of new authorities. These new authorities now constitute for large parts of the world the 'world come of age', the primary one of which is the modern state. In the scene from *Schindler's List* referenced earlier, one sees on display all the elements of the modern state: The control exerted through bureaucracy, the creation of crises (there is nothing better for the modern state than perpetual war), mass media to create worldviews, and the development of technologies that would allow states to control their populations.[99]

The modern state has to rest on a type of foundation in order to lay claim to some legitimacy, which is where ideology comes into play, for few states can move their citizens to give their lives for geopolitical power, economic gain or dominance. Ideology supplies the justification for the way the state operates. Bonhoeffer offers a remarkably contemporary assessment when, in addressing the power of ideologies in *Discipleship*, he describes: 'The driving restlessness of the group of disciples who do not want to accept any limitation on their effectiveness,

---

[99] There is an interesting aspect of this in *Ethics* where Bonhoeffer writes about the distinction between the natural and the unnatural. He says that the unnatural seeks to extend itself through organizing functions which themselves seek to control and efface the organic dimensions of life, pp. 176–78. This ties into what Zygmunt Bauman argues in *Modernity and the Holocaust* (Ithaca, NY: Cornell University Press, 1989), 17ff., when he says that it is modernity that made the Holocaust possible because there were no effective means to prevent it. This is due in no small part to the shape rational control of the world assumes when it extends its power: 'I also suggest that it was the spirit of instrumental rationality, and its modern, bureaucratic form of institutionalization, which had made the Holocaust-style solutions not only possible, but eminently "reasonable"– and increased the probability of their choice.'

and their zeal, which does not respect resistance, confuses the word of the gospel with a conquering idea. An idea requires fanatics, who neither know nor respect resistance.'[100]

The issue of how ideology can do so much damage recurs in Bonhoeffer's writings. In *Ethics* he discusses how the responsible person thinks clearly about the consequences of her decision, but the ideologues don't have this wisdom or care. For the sake of ideological purity, the consequences of actions taken in the world are not thought about, or carefully considered. The resultant damage from this creates the conditions for more pain and suffering in the world because 'Those who act on ideology consider themselves justified by their idea.'[101]

In the 'world come of age' it is not the religion but the idea that becomes the absolute, functioning in its own way to make ultimate claims over all those under its sphere of influence. Because ideologies assume the status they do, they perpetuate the maintenance of a type of social order by legitimating the political powers from which that order emerges. In this way, secularization has led to the replacement of religion with ideology as authoritative for social structuring because now it functions to locate temporal and contingent realities in the transcendence of the Idea.[102]

This is the shadow side of humankind's autonomy. What Bonhoeffer knew very well in his life was that the political order seeks to control the conscience of all those under its sway. Because the Nazi regime was so horrifically efficient at this for some time, we lose sight of the fact that the same dynamics of social control operate in contemporary life as well. In fact, in some way the utter demonization of the Nazi regime serves to cloak the very real problems with any political system that seeks hegemonic power. No matter how bad things get, no matter how many people are killed in the name of a particular ideology, we can always say, 'Well, at least it wasn't as bad as the Nazis.' In thinking this we become somehow immunized from seeing that the same dynamics

[100] *Discipleship*, p. 173.

[101] *Ethics*, pp. 225–26. His warnings against ideology apply to all along the political and religious spectrums as well. Even Christians can abstract the words of Jesus from Christ's life in the Triune God, thus having these words made an ideology for revolution or the maintenance of the status quo. See also pp. 263–72.

[102] I am thinking here of the way that the state came to assume the power it does in the modern world. It is no accident that the rise of science as authoritative for the West was accompanied by the rise of the modern state as the prominent form of social order. Once science had reduced God to filling in the gaps of human knowledge the state became the only institution big enough to stand in for divine governance of human life.

of control, violence and manipulation that marked that order have the potential of being manifested in every other political structure on the planet unless true diligence is maintained.

As it is, the elites work hard to maintain their social control, and in so doing create the conditions for impersonality, alienation and social maintenance. The result is that the secular teleology mentioned earlier becomes the guiding factor for ordering human life away from questions about how we should construct life, to ways in which life can be more efficiently managed: 'Put somewhat differently, early political theorists shifted the whole focus of the discussion away from the question of how we *ought* to live together in society toward the pragmatic consideration of how human beings actually do live together, and how this behavior can be effectively *managed.*'[103]

Bonhoeffer understood that religion had been eradicated from this process unless it was used to shore up the reigning political orders. Yet the movement of ideology to take religion's place has profoundly shaped the 'world come of age'. This occurs precisely because in a secular society religion loses its ability to shape the world, other than to legitimize the prevailing worldviews. Another irony is that ideology is as controlling and absolute as religion ever was, but those moderns who attack religion are blind to the reality that they have replaced one absolute with another, which stands on equally shaky ground and generates more violence because of its very technologies than the religion they so deplore.

What Bonhoeffer so astutely recognized in his writing is that ideologues perform the same type of social maintenance by legitimating or seizing political power necessary to dominate the way reality gets narrated. It is a cheap substitute for faith in that regard, but people are mobilized and serve the ideologies of the state with their very lives. The world of modernity and its various permutations of the state seek to wrest the consciences of those under its domain to their ends so that the masses will become fodder for maintenance of social control. And this dynamic applies to many political orders of the modern world. Ideologies create the conditions for impersonality and alienation. The individual dissipates as so much smoke at the service of larger causes like 'patriotism' by those who have the power to define this term.

Consider what we are currently experiencing with the emergence of the modern state and its attendant technologies. The ability to shape

---

[103] Craig M. Gay, *The Way of the (Modern) World or, Why it is Tempting to Live as if God Doesn't Exist* (Grand Rapids, MI: W. B. Eerdmans, 1998), pp. 56–57.

the reality of the modern world has never been more liquid than with the rise of modern media. What before would have taken months to achieve through writing now takes minutes though electronic means. The saturation provided by radio, television and, most recently, the invention of the computer, provides those who control such technologies the power to control society. This comes not only through the technologies of control such as data-mining and electronic surveillance, but also through the media's ability to shape the realities we most strongly believe in, or conversely, to undermine meanings that oppose the status quo. The interesting aspect of this is that oftentimes the media serve as partners in creating the reality the powers seek to construct, so that it becomes a self-perpetuating cycle.[104]

In the 'world come of age' people believe that they are responding to reality in accordance with the way that things really are, but in fact they can be creating reality according to how they wish it to be.[105] Perhaps it has always been thus. We just have a better grasp on how it all functions. But with this desire to create the world also comes the necessity of keeping people from peeking too closely behind the curtain or questioning the assumptions we are trying to instill. This is where the world of science and technology can be so valuable.

With the technologies of control presently available, and the alphabet soup of bureaucracies that emerge to support and direct them, the way is prepared for nation-states to assume vast control over the populations they ostensibly serve. Done on a vast scale in Bonhoeffer's day, we are seeing a multiplication of intensity in our own. Modern government can expand its reach into our lives by manipulating and manufacturing crises because it alone has the power to respond to these crises.

---

[104] Take, for example, this exchange found in Ron Suskind's article about the Bush administration 'Without a Doubt' in the *New York Times* magazine of 17 October 2004. In this discussion, a member of the White House was talking to Suskind about his being a part of the news community that reported on world events. He said: 'That's not the way the world really works anymore. We're an empire now, and when we act we create our own reality. And while you're studying that reality, judiciously as you will, we'll act again, creating other new realities which you can study too, and that's how things will sort out. We're history's actors . . . and you, all of you will be left to just study what we do.'

[105] This, of course, seems patently ridiculous to those caught up in this dynamic. We don't create terrorist attacks, we tell ourselves, we only respond to the realities present. The road that led to those attacks, however, is never examined in order to pursue a course of action that might mitigate the violence in the future. Thus our present actions become the grounds upon which future reality is created. For all our supposed autonomy we act in surprisingly constricted ways.

This is a power we offer the state because most often we find our-selves becoming fearful of the world that we ourselves have shaped. There are legitimate grounds for the state to protect its citizens and maintain social order, however, what we are currently facing in the 'world come of age' are states that under the public concerns of social order often pursue private goals that serve the interests of the elite. Because of this distinction persons oftentimes rightly regard the state's agenda with suspicion. Unfortunately, resources squandered for the extension of power and influence while citizens go hungry raise ques-tions about the state's aims.

It's All About the Money

This is why a close look reveals that nation-states do not exist solely for the purposes of pursuing ideology, rather it appears that ideology is put in the service of other forces that are as inexorable in their own way as the state. Thus we come to the other pillar upon which the world of modernity is created, economics, or more precisely, capital-ism and its markets. It is the market that constitutes one of the most significant and influential forces driving modernity today. The logics of the marketplace usually operate on the basis that the individuals that exist are quantifiable and rented. The greatest concern of the firm or company is that you are dependable, loyal and predictable. The corpo-ration is not concerned about your private life, save as it impacts your ability to perform on the job. You can be whatever religion you want, but only in ways that are easily accommodated (food, dress, observance).

The market does not really want a rigorous expression of religion in the public sector. This is another reason why religion in the modern world gets fenced into the private domain, and is always messy when it intrudes into the marketplace. In fact, one of the most interesting aspects of capitalist economics is that it is based on the death of God: 'This is no secret revelation; some of the key architects of capitalist economics fully understood this and stated it publicy.'[106]

---

[106] See, for example, this quote, 'The "death of God" had produced a great upsurge of cheerfulness among those we would now call social scientists. "The desire to put mankind in the saddle is the mainspring of most economic study", wrote Alfred Marshall in the 1890's; the implication being that some men were at least intellectually and morally equal to their post-theological tasks.' Robert Skidelsky, *John Maynard Keynes: The Economist as Saviour, 1920–1937* (London: Penguin, 1992), p. 170. See, also, Stephen Long, *The Goodness of God: Theology, Church, and the Social Order* (Grand Rapids, MI: Brazos Press, 2001), p. 249.

We do find that the more integrated we become in the logics and rationalities that shape the contemporary world such as the market, the less able we become to truly recognize what another way of being in the world would look like. Being absorbed into the 'world come of age' renders modern humanity unable to truly grasp its captivity to the objectification of human life that modern capitalism creates. Capitalism creates such a vast web of institutions and structures, all oriented to certain ends, that we never really question, that it possesses the enormous power to shape and form our very identities.

In an odd way, this perversely mirrors Bonhoeffer's statement about God no longer being seen as a stop-gap. Once we function very well on our own, God becomes superfluous. In the matter of economics we find that markets function much better if they are devoid of any religion: '. . . the peculiar genius of the market mechanism lies precisely in its ability to coordinate peaceful and ordered economic exchange *in the absence* of consensus on religious matters of substance.'[107] Fidelity to the economic order almost necessitates the absence of loyalty to anything higher.

The good life becomes definable in terms of economics, not in terms of the community of persons who participate in life. The formation of character can become sacrificed on the altar of financial expediency. If religion were to be invited into the space of financial exchange the market could not exist under the present conditions. It would be considered 'irrational' to order our lives on the basis of religion. In fact, this is the response if someone mentions something remotely religious in economic affairs. If we possess a rational system that purportedly works so well in the service of enlightened self-interest why would we introduce an irrational element like religion

---

[107] Gay, p. 174. This is an area that is attracting much attention these days as theologians seek to define what the intersection of economics and theology looks like. The treatments of this area range from those from the Radical Orthodoxy expression identified with John Milbank such as D. Stephen Long, who deals extensively with this issue in his *Divine Economy: Theology and the Market* (London and New York: Routledge, 2000) to Rebecca Todd Peters, *In Search of the Good Life: An Ethics of Globalization* (New York, NY: Continuum, 2004). My purpose here is not to assess the different arguments, merely to point out that the trajectory that modernity has followed in its coming of age has led us to a certain type of understanding about humankind and its formation by the forces that shape us. We will always have an economic structure of some sort with markets. The question is whether the present shape of economic structure serves to enhance the life of those on the planet.

into the equation? As Bonhoeffer understood, we manage our affairs perfectly well without God.

But the true concern here is that the individualism present in our current form of capitalism erodes the potential for building an authentic sense of community among persons. We may create a false sense of community through national and ethnic appeals to keep workers unaware of a larger corporate identity with others in the world, but ultimately modern capitalism lacks the ability to maintain the emotional bonds that would serve to bind human persons to one another: 'Where individualism rules alone, it will make society into a mechanistic social apparatus in which all are fixed on their own interests, and face each other in competition, or at a cool distance.'[108]

Thus our identities in the 'world come of age' are constructed by consumption. Our things shape us. This car is you, this house is you, you are not important to me unless you possess a certain type of thing with a certain type of name. The market shapes us in terms of our character and aesthetics, even to the point where we become something completely different as persons than what we have been.

By this I mean that for the citizens of cultures completely situated within contemporary capitalism's grasp we are no longer shaped by interaction with the larger community of others as persons. Indeed other person's claims on my life are negated to the extent they interfere with my 'right' to a certain lifestyle. In our absorption by the market, we become impersonal to others because our lives become defined by how efficiently we serve the system of financial exchange. We are no longer individuals of unique worth or concern, rather we are reduced to individuals who get to have the freedom to choose what we consume.

This creates the illusion that we have freedom. Indeed, the marketing campaigns of more than one corporation have manipulated a willing population into buying a certain product because it offered us 'freedom'. But what freedom is truly present when we are afforded the opportunity to choose between false, ephemeral choices? We do create a self that concerns itself with individuality more than community, but this individual is all the more susceptible to manipulation. If we are what we consume, then we become shaped by all those aspects of

---

[108] Heinz Eduard Tödt, *Authentic Faith: Bonhoeffer's Theological Ethics in Context*, eds. Ernest-Albert Scharffenorth and Glen Harold Stassen, trans. David Stassen and Ilse Tödt (Grand Rapids, MI: W. B. Eerdmans, 2007), p. 60.

capitalism that seek to define humankind in just such a way to make persons more pliable to marketing.

Western individualism is shaped by a certain way of understanding autonomy. One can argue that this was, in no small measure, unleashed with Luther's preposterous performance at the Diet of Worms, when in the presence of all arrayed powers of church and state, he appealed to his conscience. Enshrined in the idea of the priesthood of the believer is a subjectivity which does begin to shape the life of human beings. But what type of humanity emerges from a world that defines persons solely on the basis of their utility to the function of corporate entities, dissolving individuals into impersonal objects to be manipulated?

The great irony of our day is that acceptance of the current form of the great powers of economy and state as necessary leads to people who, while celebrating their freedom, are less free than they realize. The more individual they become on the conditions that the state and market allow, the more cut-off from community they are. And the more removed from community we become, the less able we are to resist those very forces of ideology and economics that exercise such subtle power to shape and control us.

In fact, the 'world come of age' that we are creating is fashioning a fascist architecture of the soul in the service to abstractions like state and economics that take certain concrete forms, most often secured by violence. We close ourselves into the very prisons we have built and then tell ourselves we are authentic selves, but the selves we have created are themselves but wisps that appear and disappear as circumstances warrant.[109]

The market becomes such an irresistible force that it must be continually fed. Its movement through our lives is so much more pervasive because of the technologies that presently exist. We are moving at hyper-speed as all identities are being swept away. The market has its own logic and that logic is absolutist. Market functioning in its present configurations will influence nations, peoples and identities by the creation of new desires and needs, environments, and a different type of humanity. But there is ample reason to believe that we will not be

---

[109] Two places where an account of the creation of the modern self can be found are Charles Taylor, *The Sources of the Self: The Making of Modern Identity* (Cambridge, MA: Harvard University Press, 1989) and Kenneth J. Gergen, *The Saturated Self: Dilemmas of Identity in Contemporary Life* (New York, NY: Basic Books, 1991).

able to sustain the environment we live in if we continue along the path that modern capitalism is leading us on.

The market also expresses its own ecumenicity, for we are all joined by the narratives the market creates for us. Globalization has taken local narratives and extended them over the world: "'Utopia," says the president of Nabisco Corporation, is "One world of homogeneous consumption . . . [I am] looking forward to the day when Arabs and Americans, Latins and Scandinavians will be munching Ritz crackers as enthusiastically as they already drink Coke and brush their teeth with Colgate."[110] It is to be seen whether the hand not holding Coke and Ritz crackers will be holding the barrel of a gun to keep others from getting their soda and crackers.

The market seeks to create a community that serves particular ends, but whether this is the ecumenicity of desire for a community able to transcend the boundaries that the state seeks to maintain is doubtful. Even more dubious, for those who seek to resist this movement of a 'world come of age' on the grounds of Christian faith is whether the type of community engendered by capitalism can offer help to those most in need of a community of peace. A communion of Ritz crackers becomes a poor substitute for the table of peace engendered by the bread and wine of the crucified Jesus.

In the face of this when we look at apocalyptic literature in the Bible we may not be too surprised to find that the sign that stands above all signs of the evil thing, the mark of the Beast, is the mark that allows one to buy or sell. We shall have more to say about this later, but for now, the type of Christianity that Bonhoeffer sees as able to resist the 'world come of age' would understand apocalyptic literature as being generated by those outside the margins, the ones not able to participate fully in economic self-determination, the ones 'from below'. In our day, it is certainly those whose existence is lived on the boundaries who most urgently feel the concerns for human survival at risk through the power of the market.[111]

Bonhoeffer was not able to completely flesh out the ways in which the monopoly of the church had been broken by the forces unleashed by the Reformation, though he had a pretty good idea that we live in

---

[110] William Cavanaugh, *Theopolitical Imagination: Discovering the Liturgy as a Political Act in an Age of Global Consumerism* (Edinburg: T & T Clark, 2002), pp. 105–06. See also Benjamin Barber's *Jihad vs. McWorld* (New York, NY: Ballantine Books, 1996).

[111] Larry Rasmussen points this out in his book, *Dietrich Bonhoeffer's Significance for North Americans*, p. 76.

an age after Christendom. The unitary power of the church no longer exists and though religion occupies space and many participate in its comforts, the reality of God has dissipated to such a space that all social orders operate on the basis of a practical atheism. *Etsi deus non daretur,* indeed.

The modern world works on the basis of a certain type of understanding that values experience, rationality, the immediate and probability as guiding factors in constructing our world. These habits of thought, shored up by the pragmatic success of disciplines like science, become the touchstones whereby we make our reality. These aspects of the maturation of humankind create us as souls that lack the imagination or faith to extend the boundaries of our social arrangements beyond what the spaces of our known existence look like.

This creates a certain gravity that sucks all into its vortex. We are both defining and becoming defined by our own creations, but these have delivered to us a world that is constituted by superficiality, and destruction for many who do not live within the walls of power. With our technology we have created more knowledge than ever before, but we lack wisdom. And, oddly, here is where Bonhoeffer returns to offer us insight. Because the maturation of the world, while not to be resisted by religious appeals, also needs to be called into question.

Bonhoeffer himself had just this in mind when he writes on 18 July 1944:

> When we speak of God in a 'non-religious' way, we must speak of him in such a way that the godlessness of this world is not in some way concealed, but rather revealed, and thus exposed to an unexpected light. The world that has come of age is more godless, and perhaps for that very reason nearer to God, than the world before its coming of age.[112]

In saying this Bonhoeffer does not mean to resist the principalities and powers by addressing humankind in its weaknesses or vulnerabilities, rather he believed that the world's coming of age opens a ground whereby Christian faith may, without manipulative appeals to guilt, question what the coming of age has brought us. Only now this interrogation of the world can take place under the auspices of a faith that does not occupy a place of privilege vis-à-vis the world.

Previously, Bonhoeffer had reflected on the ways in which Christianity had been displaced from the public space of the world and reduced

---

[112] *LPP*, p. 362.

to the sphere of the inner, private world of the self, as if this move could somehow or the other protect the viability of Christianity. He had some trenchant observations to make about the process that follows this move, especially in the way that something like psychotherapy or existentialist philosophy seeks to exploit this retreat to inwardness by showing humans how weak and vulnerable they truly are. He writes:

> Regarded theologically, the error is twofold. First it is thought that a man can be addressed as a sinner only after his weaknesses and meannesses have been spied out. Secondly, it is thought that a man's essential nature consists of his utmost and most intimate background; that is defined as his 'inner life', and it is precisely in those secret human places that God is to have his domain![113]

Bonhoeffer goes on to comment that this seems entirely wrong. On the one hand, humankind is certainly sinful, but the place to address this is precisely where humankind manifests its greatest strengths, not its weaknesses or vulnerabilities of the flesh ('were Goethe and Napoleon sinners because they weren't always faithful husbands?'). No, it is the place of greatest strength and thus of greatest hubris that humans must be confronted. It is in those spaces of great world creating power that the self-destruction of the 'world come of age' becomes all too concrete. The process of world creating that Bonhoeffer reflected on in Tegel offers us a perspective on the world that clears the ground for a new engagement about what reality looks like.

How does a religionless Christianity respond to the political and economic orders that presently dominate the world? It is a world that seeks to create all in its image, to eradicate all difference, all resistance, that stands as the apex of the 'world come of age'. This is where the word of the gospel needs to be spoken. The laying hold of world shaping power by those whose hubris allows all other human claims to become invisible is the place where the true sinfulness of the world come of age is manifest. These are the spaces that Christianity must address:

> I therefore want to start from the premise that God shouldn't be smuggled into some secret place, but that we should frankly recognize that the world, and people, have come of age, that we shouldn't run man down in his worldliness, but confront him with God at his strongest point, that we should give up all

[113] *LPP*, p. 345.

clerical tricks and not regard psychotherapy and existential philosophy as God's pioneers.[114]

The way in which Christianity does this and the form of Christianity that is capable of challenging the 'world come of age' will be the focus of our attention in much of this work, but for now we must turn to the phenomenon of religion to try and discern whether Christian faith can itself ever truly be 'religionless'. It is a lingering irony that in the 'world come of age' religion, which was supposed to die a quiet death, has, in fact, emerged to present one of the greatest challenges to the peace that state and market so desire.

[114] *LPP*, p. 346.

Chapter 4

THE ECLIPSE OF RELIGION? BONHOEFFER AND RELIGIONLESS CHRISTIANITY

The smoke rises from the rubble of a bombed building in New York City, Jerusalem, Belfast or Baghdad. Chaos, dead bodies, havoc and the sight of passions inflamed as chants are yelled and gunshots fill the air. And somewhere in the world where these things take place you just know that the name of God, or Allah, or Shiva is going to be invoked. The images are ubiquitous on our televisions and in our media. We live in a world scarred by religious violence. It is difficult for the astute observer to look at religion today and not feel the shadow of fear and loathing. The world suffers religiously inspired violence, where words like 'infidel' and 'crusade' are invoked with the deep passion fueled by the memories of centuries of injustice and grievance. These passions have created a world that is torn by disputes among religious communities.

In the march to autonomy we explored in the last chapter, religion was in some senses meant to disappear beneath the waves of rationality that the secular order constructed for itself to secure its power. This appeal to rationality was accompanied by the myth of the clean slate that saw in the rise of rationality the means to sweep away traditions, especially religious ones, and start from scratch. This rationality would be unencumbered with the superstitions of religion. After humankind had attained its autonomy from the forces of superstition and taken responsibility for itself, religion was supposed to quietly disappear from the stage, consigned as a relic of an age long forgotten. This havoc that we see in our time was supposed to have vanished in the march to adulthood.[115]

In the 'world come of age' religion and all its accoutrements, God, salvation, heaven, hell, etc., should have long ago been sent to the sidelines. The celebration of secularity that many of Bonhoeffer's interpreters embraced back in the 1960s has turned like a bad dream to apocalyptic visions of falling skyscrapers and exploding bodies. Religion, it seems, was only biding its time, waiting for another of its many turns on the stage. The slow domestication of religion seems to have been yet another secular fantasy.[116]

Of course, part of this scenario was being written in a cultural world where the most sophisticated believed that religion had long

[115] See Stephan Toulmin's account of this process in *Cosmopolis: The Hidden Agenda of Modernity* (New York, NY: Free Press, 1990), p. 175.

[116] It is crucial at this point to call attention to the fact that the word 'religion' is itself a contested term that in the present day contains no one accepted definition. Some of the strongest questions about the way this term has been used as a means of ideological control and manipulation come from those like Timothy Fitzgerald who argues that the use of the term 'religion' was accompanied by the rise of the type of rationality under discussion. See, for example, Timothy Fitzgerald, *The Ideology of Religious Studies* (New York, Oxford: Oxford University Press, 2000). He is not the only one and the fact that religion has been used for ideological purposes is not that novel a thought. When one follows out the history of the concept, there are many interpretations from which to choose, but for our purposes, the word came to stand for an interior state of beliefs and ideas that one believed about such things as the sacred or the transcendent. The emergence of the word corresponded with the decline of the church as the particular locus of the practice of religion as a virtue that directs one to God (see William Cavanaugh's discussion of religion in its early usage and the ways in which St. Thomas Aquinas used it to signify a practice of virtue, *Theopolitical Imagination*, p. 32).

Wilfred Cantwell Smith also contends that the word 'religion' undergoes significant revision of meaning in the rise of modernity. It shows up in Marsilio Ficino as a universal human impulse that is common to all and assumes the dimensions of the true essence that is implanted in every human heart. This later mutates again when Hugo Grotius contends that religion in some ways is a system of beliefs or propositions which teaches us about God. It is about this time that the plural 'religions' comes into use. The truth is that when the word 'religion' was used by Calvin, Ficino or Grotius it had very different meanings. In this way, Fitzgerald is right because the gravity of a universal notion of religion pulls everything within its orbit. All religion becomes interpreted by the way it conforms to supposedly universal moral or metaphysical truths. Though this is not within our task in this text, religion becomes a domesticated series of beliefs that serve the state as an instrument of control within its own realm. It also means the colonization of others whose religious beliefs do not conform to the knowable truths of the dominant culture. As long as religion serves the cause of the state, then the state 'tolerates' it, but if religion were to assume some other dimension, say of one that argues that the virtues of religion should actually be lived practices, then religion must be removed from public expression for the common good. This is a long and complex since served its purpose and new substitutes would be ample to supply the human spirit with sustenance in its search for meaning. What science did not take care of, psychology, politics, or a host of other secular substitutes would. We were told at the dawn of the world to come that religion was a projection of human emotions and concerns that we focused on an external object, God, which did not exist.

Religion, and its ultimate language symbol, God, was the unconscious wish of fragile human beings to create a world of meaning. In his critique of religion Sigmund Freud wrote:

> We say to ourselves: It would be very nice if there were a God, who was both Creator of the world and a benevolent providence, if there were a moral world order and a future life, but at the same time it is very odd that this is all just as we should wish it ourselves. And, it would be still odder if our poor, ignorant, enslaved ancestors had succeeded in solving all these difficult riddles of the universe.[117]

Those like Sigmund Freud and Ludwig Feuerbach offered a critique that simply accorded with the facts. Humans tend to create God, the gods, in their own image. Bonhoeffer offered one of his assessments here: 'Both the most grandiose and the frailest of all human attempts to reach the eternal out of fear and unrest in the human heart is religion.'[118] In this, he can agree with religion's critics, but the issue for Bonhoeffer is can he find a way to escape this gravity? Is there a way he can secure his faith from the truth of this critique? If religion is merely the human writ large, how can Christianity escape that critique? As an assistant pastor in Barcelona, Bonhoeffer believed that religion as the human attempt to attain the divine can lead to problems. He can agree with the critics in this sense: 'The religious path from human beings to God leads to the idol of our hearts which we have formed after our own image. Neither knowledge, nor morality, nor religion leads to God.'[119]

---

history, but we will find some of the consequences for our purposes later. See Wilfred Cantwell Smith, *The Meaning and End of Religion* (New York, NY: The Macmillan Company, 1962), p. 19.

[117] Sigmund Freud, *The Future of an Illusion*, trans. and ed. James Strachey (New York, NY: W. W. Norton, 1961), p. 42.

[118] Bethge, p. 113.

[119] Wüstenberg, p. 3.

A cursory glance at humankind provides us with ample evidence that this is true. So much of what we label with the term 'religion' appears to be the hopeless attempt to root ourselves and all the extensions of self found in family, nation or state, within the absolute. Once religion is rooted there anything becomes possible in the name of God, even the death and annihilation of others who do not share our particular idea of the absolute. The gods are seldom found on the sides of our enemies after all.

Religion creates the conditions not only for individuals to wear the cloak of self-righteousness, but entire cultures to don it as well. Then everything becomes justified on the basis of transcendent command. God is easily employed for privileging my tribe, my community, my culture. Thus my society acquires the authority of the ultimate where life is rooted not in the vagaries of history, but in the solidity of the absolute.

In this sense, religion has the potential to construct the deepest part of myself, the core of my identity, for my identity is shaped and formed by the host of social arrangements I find myself within. The depth of this is so deep, the power of this so vast, that we accept the constructs of our culture as self-evident truths. When sociologists write of religion as constructing a 'sacred canopy' over society they are indicating that all the dynamics that go into shaping culture are shaping our deepest identities as well, and tying those identities to the transcendent. This identification can be so deep that any questioning of those identities of culture or self, either from within the culture, or outside of it, will elicit the strongest possible response, even unto violence and death. When we begin to question the most fundamental aspects of our lives, the ones that are so deeply held they are not even conscious to us, the resultant anxiety does spawn significant resistance.

Religion functions to shape and place us by the narratives it offers us. In this sense, we are narrated persons, whose worlds are shaped by the stories that we heard as we grew up in the lands of our elders. These stories locate us in the world and along with those who passed these stories onto us, tell us who we were. Religion serves to legitimate all social arrangements so that the actions we take, the beliefs we hold, our very place in the cosmos, are all placed in an authority beyond the relativities of history. The fact that religion works ideologically in this way is really not all that surprising, since it shares the same space of cultural construction that every other human creation does.

Cultural identity insinuates itself with particular force when it is tied to the sacred because it creates the conditions that can cause us to commit atrocity in God's name: 'Such sacralization of cultural identity is invaluable for the parties in conflict because it can transmute what is in fact a murder into an act of piety.'[120] Suicide bombers and Crusaders alike share this space. This has often been present in the dynamics of religion from the time we first gathered around fires in caves to tell the stories that formed us. It is God, not us, who wills the destruction of our enemies. We are comfortable with our convenient delusions. We wrap them around us to conceal ourselves from the truth that most actions undertaken in the name of God by both societies and individuals arise more from the will to power than the desire to embody God's presence.

This, of course, is difficult for the Christian to hear and is one reason why Bonhoeffer can so perplex us. He never really develops a theory of religion, nor is there a fixed place in him that one can point to and think they possess the interpretive key to Bonhoeffer's concept of religion. Some people find themselves agitated by Bonhoeffer's perspective because in some ways he tries to insulate religionless Christianity from the critique of religion offered by its cultural despisers. Even given Bonhoeffer's best efforts, it is questionable whether Christianity can ever be separated from the centuries of enculturation and relation to power that have shaped it over the course of so many centuries. In that regard, it remains a religion in the deepest sense and it is hard to distinguish some essence in Christianity that transcends the nexus of religion and culture.

Towards the end of his life when he was imprisoned in Tegel, Bonhoeffer offered such a distinction between Christianity and religion when he wrote:

> Here is the decisive difference between Christianity and all religions. Man's religiosity makes him look in his distress to the power of God in the world. God is the *deus ex machina*. The Bible directs man to God's powerlessness and suffering; only the suffering God can help. To that extent we may say the development towards the world coming of age outlined above which has done away with a false conception of God, opens up a way of seeing the God of the Bible who wins power and space in the world by his weakness. This will probably be the starting-point of our 'secular interpretation.'[121]

---

[120] Miroslav Volf, *Exclusion and Embrace: A Theological Exploration of Identity, Otherness, and Reconciliation* (Nashville, TN: Abingdon Press, 1996), p. 37.

[121] *LPP*, p. 361. In Greek and Roman drama, the *deus ex machina* was a god or literary device to resolve difficulties in a plot.

He came to this moment at the end of a life of thinking and reflecting on these issues, but the relationship between Christianity and religion was always at the centre of his thoughts. Early in his life as a pastor in Barcelona he was struggling with this issue when, in a sermon on I Corinthians 12:9 in 1928, he signalled his understanding of the distinction, proclaiming: 'With that the difference between Christianity and all other religions is clear, here is grace, there happiness, here the cross, there the crown; here God, there the human.'[122] He seems to understand at this point that Christianity itself shares a certain space with religion, but he wants to privilege it nonetheless. This is a difficult belief because, like it or not, Christianity shares the same limitations, historical conditioning and self-serving interests that all religion is influenced by. This truth would later sink in on him though.

Ralf K. Wüstenberg observes that Bonhoeffer discerned early in his career that the word *religio* entered into the lexicon of the intellectual rather than faith. Religion became a substitute for faith. Religion thus became the canvas upon which its critics can paint their works because it becomes a cultural artefact reducible to what anthropology, psychology or a host of other academic disciplines interpret it to be. Nineteenth century theological liberalism was unable to respond effectively because it, too, was captivated by religion as a human *a priori*. For theologians like Schleiermacher religion is first located within the depths of the human person and thus all theology must begin with the human and seek the innate capacity of the individual to respond to a Supreme Being.[123]

This forms the cultural context within which Bonhoeffer and one of his most important theological influences, Karl Barth, were trying to forge a new path. It was precisely the perceived deficiencies in liberal Protestant theology that drew their attention and their fire. They believed that 'the concept of religion developed by liberal theology replaced the concept of faith of Reformational theology; theology, he believes, became anthropology.'[124]

---

[122] Bethge, p. 113.

[123] See, for instance, Schleiermacher's entire approach found in *Speeches on Religion*. Trans. Richard Crouter (Cambridge: Cambridge University Press, 1992).

[124] Wüstenberg, p. 92. In 1931–1932 Bonhoeffer sees Barth's path as the way to answer Feuerbach and escape from the cultural captivity of Protestantism, but in Tegel he explores new paths that will take him away from Barth.

Barth's dialectical theology, seen most powerfully in his commentary, *The Epistle to the Romans*, is a rejection of the modern understanding of religion that the 'world come of age' had been constructing for itself since the eighteenth century, especially with the work begun by Schleiermacher. God was not a universal and inner aspect of all humanity that could be known by the right type of rationality. Bonhoeffer had been captivated by Barth's critique and resonated with it in many ways, though later on he would put his own stamp upon the matter. He was initially drawn to Barth's dialectical tensions, but ultimately he realized that Christianity walks away privileged in some way or the other unless it, too, comes under the scrutiny launched against other expressions of religion.

There are many aspects of this critique to consider. If the religious question is one that reveals far more about ourselves than it does about God, in what ways does this become manifest in human society? How does religion operate to fulfil human desire or need? One of the ways religion functions ideologically is to legitimate the political arrangements that human beings have created. Bonhoeffer knew that religion at the service of the political powers of his day was a deadly prospect, and in a sermon on 12 June 1932 in the Kaiser Wilhelm Memorial Church concerning the misuse of God's name he proclaimed:

> Or is there not concealed behind our religious trends our ungovernable urge toward . . . power – in the name of God to do what *we* want, and in the name of the Christian worldview to stir up and play people against one another?[125]

Bonhoeffer saw how easily persons are manipulated on the basis of how deeply their identity is tied to religion and how that ties a person's very existence into the nation, tribe or culture in which they internalized that religious perspective. In Germany, with a state church that was a shaper of reality for the citizen from cradle to the grave, the likelihood that political power would seek to colonize the religious dimension was a danger that most never even saw coming. The deep connection between religion and the will to power was simply missed by those who were and are now immersed in the forms of religion that legitimate one's own culture.

The shaping power of religion in its interaction with society can be subtle and tricky and appears in many different forms. Bonhoeffer wrote that Christianity as religion works to make of Jesus the divine

[125] Bethge, p. 236.

sanction of everything that exists. In this way, the Christian religion can become that social construction whereby all activities of society are translated into the realm of the sacred. If this takes place, then the conditions emerge for whatever exists to be inherently connected to the divine will because God stands behind it. The morality that exists in a society is therefore approved by God, especially that morality your particular cultural religious setting embraces.[126] It is this connection that Bonhoeffer found particularly troubling.

One particular manifestation of this type of morality has historically been the call to purity, the temptation of the self-righteous. This was the case in Germany as in the churches there were great protests against secularism and godlessness, against Catholicism, disbelief, and immorality.[127] Substitute whatever religion you don't like for 'Catholicism' and do we not hear echoes of this in our day? Is it not the secular humanists who are trying to destroy our country in the minds of some? Is it not the forces of immorality (though the moral values that are most in danger seem to be individual acts and not acts of larger communities like, say, politicians) that many religious people in America fear are corrupting our society? Is it not Muslims (or, if in a Muslim country the political powers of the West) who are the terrorists? In some communities of American society presently it is precisely the supposed godlessness of our country that is the problem. This is not just an issue in American society. Depending on the social location of your culture, society or nation there are many in religious communities that call for a more exclusionary stance against the onslaughts of the unbelievers and infidels.

This desire in the human heart for purity, to draw the boundaries between the pure and the impure, constitutes one of the most insidious marks of religion (and politics, of course). In Germany, Christianity was so eager to align itself with anything that proclaimed this purity that it fell right into the seductions of a political power that promised the church a world of purity. With religion we are allowed to make distinctions among ourselves on the basis of categories that have long

---

[126] There is an interesting section in *Ethics* where Bonhoeffer in contrast to this idea writes that the other common misunderstanding of Jesus is to make him the founder of a new ethical ideology that can be applied to the historical realm. This results in continual conflict between historical necessity and the ethic of Jesus. This is a curious idea coming from the author of *Discipleship*. For more of this see the discussion in *Ethics*, pp. 227–36.

[127] Bethge, p. 237.

been religion's stock in trade. One of the greatest of these distinctions is the one that divides the world into two categories: the forces of light and the forces of darkness. In a sermon prepared for Epiphany in 1936 Bonhoeffer made an interesting observation: 'All peoples, religions, and human beings like to talk about the victory of light over darkness. This is pagan wisdom and hope.'[128] It should go without saying that the forces of darkness are always the ones who disagree with us. Religion constructs its boundaries so tightly, however, that we seldom see the ways in which our community follows darkness as well as light.

The insidious nature of this is seen in the very logic of purity itself. It is a logic that puts all of culture to its service. Miroslav Volf comments that: 'The "will to purity" contains a whole program for arranging our social worlds – from the inner worlds of our selves to the outer worlds of our families, neighborhoods and nations. It is a dangerous program because it is a totalitarian program, governed by a logic that reduces, ejects and segregates.'[129] Can we not see the Nazi agenda revealed in this quote? The more disturbing issue though is whether this is, in fact, the inner dynamic that drives various religious communities, Christianity included.

In the dichotomy of the pure–impure we find the delusion, the lie of our own purity, our own innocence. This delusion allows us to proceed with impunity to visit any violence on those who threaten us. The attraction of religion is that we can be both idealistic and nationalistic at the same time. It allows us to believe we have cast off evil and are impenetrable to its colonization. Even worse, we engage in actions that we think will serve to secure our own moral purity. The result is worse than unbelief: 'Religion and morality represent the greatest danger for recognizing divine grace, since they bear within themselves the seed prompting us to seek our path to God ourselves.'[130]

This issue of morality as an ancillary aspect of religion was deeply on Bonhoeffer's mind throughout his life. In Bonhoeffer's day, the historical trajectory of the Christian religion had led to a theology that understood God's law to be rooted in the natural 'orders'. So, theology done under this umbrella made the case that God's creation brought forth family, state and other natural orders that were to be seen as inherently good. This was one of the fiercest fought battles

---

[128] *GS* 4.187. quoted from Wüstenberg, p. 13.
[129] Volf, p. 74.
[130] *DBW* 10:459.

between persons such as Barth and Emil Brunner. Theologically speaking, if you have internalized this belief then the state or any aspect of society is by virtue of its very existence ordered by God, and conformity and obedience to the Powers-That-Be is nothing less than a command of God.

As we look back in time, we see how destructive this was to the German nation and how the religion of Christianity actually set the table for the absolute blindness that occurred in that society. It is still true today. By the domestication of religion whatever passes for Christian faith becomes transmuted into cultural morality. Once diminished to this, the inevitable descent into a religion created by our own hands continues. The spaces between the pure and impure, the absolute and total obedience to the powers that exist, the will to power and justification for violence, all these are manifestations of religion acting as moral arbiter. Bonhoeffer believed that Christianity must be something more than the cultural constructions of whatever society it is known within. Indeed, Christianity must take its stand against the prevailing morality sometimes: 'The germ of hubris is contained in religion and morality . . . thus the Christian message is basically amoral and irreligious, however paradoxical that may sound.'[131]

This may sound highly suspect to our ears because in the America of today Christianity has become almost nothing other than a series of moral judgements. Those who work feverishly to restore 'traditional values' today most often invoke 'Judeo-Christian' religion as the only correct path to the Almighty. But their particular interpretation of Christianity seemingly blinds them to anything that would call their culturally shaped morality into question. Perhaps under scrutiny some of those moral values may be reflective of something authentically rooted in the life of God, but religion itself seeks to stamp the prevailing moral ethos with the weight of divine approval such that to even question it is regarded as an act of blasphemy. Sometimes it is not that simple.

Those voices which call so strongly for a return to 'traditional' values seem to lack the ability to critique or question the nation–state's role in the world. Because religion is defined so individualistically in our current context, the notion of a public good that serves the goods of God, or the public that extends beyond our borders, or our political affiliations, has been eclipsed by the same individualism that drives the religious ethos of American Christians today. Little rigorous discussion of religious values, save as it pertains to individual acts, is done today

[131] Bethge, p. 117.

in the public forum. The public and corporate morality that is held by those who have embraced the cultural expression of religion most often is one based upon individual acts. Moral acts are talked about in such a way that masks the political morality in play, which seems to excuse any lie, any human degradation, any deceit, as long as it is done in the name of freedom and democracy.

It is not that freedom and democracy are necessarily bad ideals, but they can be decidedly idolatrous in the hands of those who use them as cloaks for behavior that is self-serving. For example, as I write these words there is in America a raging debate over the use of torture. I cannot find in the gospels any justification for such an action and would argue that this is behaviour that must, on Christian grounds, be condemned. The shame of it is that there will be Christians who will support it if their government says it is right to do so. Or worse, they will choose to ignore what is being done in their name.[132]

It is this preoccupation with the individual at the expense of the larger community that was so discomforting to Bonhoeffer. It is the interior, subjective and individual aspects that are so prevalent in society today, but this concern for individual salvation has become one of the greatest problems for contemporary Protestant faith. Bonhoeffer proclaims in a sermon from 1935: 'We must finally get away from the notion that the gospel is concerned with the salvation of the soul of the individual, or with showing the way from the despair of the sinner to the sinner's blessedness.'[133] When Christianity roots itself here,

---

[132] One small example of this comes from Jane Mayer who has provided a look inside the use of torture, rendition and black sites used by the United States government. In an account on the New Yorker magazines website she recounts the following:

> The C.I.A.'s interrogation program is remarkable for its mechanistic aura. 'It's one of the most sophisticated, refined programs of torture ever,' an outside expert familiar with the protocol said. 'At every stage, there was a rigid attention to detail. Procedure was adhered to almost to the letter. There was top–down quality control, and such a set routine that you get to the point where you know what each detainee is going to say, because you've heard it before. It was almost automated. People were utterly dehumanized. People fell apart. It was the intentional and systematic infliction of great suffering masquerading as a legal process. It is just chilling.' http://newyorker.com/reporting/2007/08/13/070813fa_mayer?currentPage=1.

What Christian can say that this is not an obscenity that calls out for judgement? We are placing ourselves in the position of losing our souls by allowing this to slip into the realm of efficient bureaucracy.

[133] GS, 4.202, quoted from Wüstenberg, p. 13.

when the ultimate goal is to cultivate the salvation of one's own soul at the cost of the world, then it is doomed to be nothing more than a tool in the hands of whoever is versed enough in religious rhetoric to manipulate persons through fears and desires.

This is what religion can do; it divides life, persons, the world, into the spheres of the sacred and the profane, the spiritual and the secular, the saved and the damned, and perhaps most insidiously, the good and the evil. Thus we can respond to others on the basis of the way that we categorize them. The exclusions and the brutalities we visit on others can be excused because they are not part of the chosen ones. Those captured by the religious impulse can read their sacred texts and see justification for the destruction of their enemies. The profane must be destroyed, the evil overcome.

Even worse, when I see myself justified by God I am able to engage in all types of evil because I am secure in the fact that my intentions are honourable. This is one of the great problems of religion. Because it works in the arena of absolutes, religion allows for anything in the name of the good. Bonhoeffer was struggling with this aspect of religion as well during the period he was writing his text on ethics. But he does point out that those who serve the absolute often miss the fact that '"absolute good" is capable, to an even greater extent, of provoking nothing less than evil.'[134] This results in one of those tragic dimensions of human life that works to our harm.

One of the greatest blind spots human beings have results from the fact that well meaning action is often undertaken with the most stunning naiveté. The blindness of idealism and acting in a situation from ideological absolutism can result in great evil. Religion often plays a role in this because it so easily dichotomizes the world along the lines mentioned above. When we are able to create simplistic dualisms through our religion without a rigorous examination of our own behaviour in the world we are capable of anything in the name of the perceived good.

SAVED – FOR WHAT?

One of the great goods of religion is salvation. The idea of soteriology occurs in many different religious expressions though this means different things to those who are defining the word. In the most general sense, it does indicate the desire to be saved from something that

[134] *Ethics*, p. 222.

threatens either the individual or the community. It can take the form of being delivered from eternal death, or from the earthly hell our enemies seek to unleash upon us.

Certainly much of the religiously fueled conflict we see in the world today is generated by a desire of some in Islam to be saved from the pollutions of the West, as well as the desire of some in Christianity to be saved from the Islamic 'Other'. When you look at the situation in the Middle East today it looks like the religious narratives of all three monotheistic traditions are at work informing the efforts of religious persons trying to 'save' their society from those who lack 'true' faith, even though the secular orders of the state may not be as concerned about saving society from religious pollution as they are in saving their space of privilege.

When my salvation becomes a matter of saving my culture, or keeping myself pure, I have entered into what Bonhoeffer called 'pagan wisdom'. If my religious self is seeking to maintain purity over against those who would defile me and my society I am allowed to engage in behaviour that in other circumstances would be reprehensible. Persons usually don't bomb innocent citizens with suicide attacks because they are utterly sadomasochistic, they do so because in many instances their God, or the particular community that has taught them about God, tells them this is what God desires in order to remove the pollutions from their midst.

In another way, religion can become a sickness unto death because the temptation is to root the religious impulse for salvation in the transcendent and interior space. It becomes easier to ignore the life of God immersed in the world because we become the central focus in the drama of life, not God. If I find myself with a preoccupation concerning my own soul I will also be most concerned about the state of another's soul more than the total state of their life. If I am not attentive to the totality of another's existence I become blind to whether they are unlawfully imprisoned, deaf to the cry of a hungry stomach, and complicit in their destruction through war. Preoccupation with my own piety can result in a neglect of all other realities which Christian faith commands us to address. In a quote that echoes his earlier sermon Bonhoeffer writes: 'We must finally rid ourselves of the notion that the issue . . . is the personal salvation of the individual soul . . . In such religious individual methodology human beings themselves remain the central focus.'[135]

---

[135] *GS*, 4.202, Wüstenberg, p. 78.

At the end of his life, Bonhoeffer sat in his prison cell and pondered where his religious ethos had brought him. A culture blinded to being used by political powers for unholy purposes, a preoccupation with the individual soul to the detriment of the larger community and the life of God immersed within the world, and a horrible seduction of Christianity that had turned it into a tool of pogrom, ethnic cleansing and death-dealing terror. No wonder he wanted to find a way to negate religion. Sitting in the midst of one of Europe's most religious cultures he clearly discerns the moral and spiritual bankruptcy of Christianity as his country knew it. Was there any hope for a religion that had become so vacated of anything resembling the spirit of Jesus Christ? If there was such a hope it was going to emerge only when Christianity freed itself from religion.

CHRISTIANITY WITHOUT RELIGION?

Bonhoeffer was probing these tensions from the earliest writings of *Sanctorum Communio*, through *Discipleship* and *Life Together*. He wondered how the Christian faith can move away from the temptations of religion to be tied to national or ethnic identity, or psychological need. During this time, he is also trying to make sense of the ways in which Jesus becomes true concrete reality within the community of faith. In the midst of the manifold failures of the church, it was hard for him to discern the ways in which Christianity exhibits faithfulness to anything other than itself.

These failures were made particularly acute with the church's failure to respond to the political situation it found itself in with the rise of the National Socialists. When Hitler came to power in January of 1933 he moved quickly to consolidate power through the passing of laws and the seduction of the church. His handling of both Catholic and Protestant churches led to the utter collapse of those communities as effective centres of real resistance to the evil within Germany. The church in Germany was co-opted because Hitler would only offer support to the extent that they supported him. The true shame is that whenever this type of support is offered to the church in return for its silence the church, for the most part, has taken the deal.

Bonhoeffer saw that the choice was going to be a stark one for the German people:

> It is becoming increasingly clear to me that what we're going to get is a long, popular, national church whose nature cannot any longer be reconciled with

Christianity and that we must be prepared to enter upon entirely new paths which we will have to thread. The question really is: Germanism or Christianity?[136]

Bonhoeffer had believed early on that the church could stand for something other than its own cultural privilege. In this, he was guided by a uniquely christocentric vision that caused the revelation of God in Jesus to mitigate our desire to make of God the empty vessel into which we pour all our desires, wishes and fears. In his context, he believed that religion needed to be unmasked in order to reveal the agendas that used it and its adherents for evil purposes. But, it was not just the pressure from the National Socialist regime that caused Bonhoeffer to pursue the type of Christology he did.

In his earliest writings, he was dealing with the provincialism to which Christ's teachings had succumbed. At issue is how Christ often ends up serving the parochial interests of society and not the larger issue of God's reign. Our continuing attempts to make God fit our particular community's interests, such as when we invoke the just war theory, or shape the idea of what 'traditional' morality looks like, shows that we have fallen prey to the seductions of religion. Whatever the merits of the just war theory in its original context, the fact is that today it has become in the hands of the ruling elites a way of putting the veneer of righteousness on political means of domination. Few leaders in American history have taken the nation to war without seeking to invoke the Almighty's blessing. Likewise, very few who advocate violence from within religious communities that are not state supported do so without claiming God's blessing. It is the bane of religion.

Bonhoeffer was struggling with a political order that ruthlessly sought to convince its citizens that its perspective, its agenda, was the only one that could restore the nation's pride and place in the world. In this the Christians of Germany were totally on board. They wanted to recover the prestige and national pride lost after the Treaty of Versailles and so they were not aware of the way that religion served the interests of its cultural masters. Even worse in the case of Christianity is the betrayal of Jesus who, in the hands of the Nazis, becomes the nebulous spiritual leader of a national cult, malleable in the hands of the political elite.

[136] Bethge, p. 302, *DBW* 12: 117–18.

Sitting in his prison cell and clearly discerning the future of his nation, Bonhoeffer was wrestling with the fact that Christian faith had proven not only impotent in the struggle with the National Socialists, it had proven complicit. Bonhoeffer saw in this that Christianity was not immune from all those critiques of religion that he had earlier penned. It was the realization that Christianity exhibited all the weaknesses of religion that caused Bonhoeffer to proclaim from his prison cell in a letter written to Bethge on 21 November 1943: 'Don't be alarmed; I shall not come out of here a *homo religiosus*! On the contrary, my fear and distrust of "religiosity" have become greater than ever here.'[137]

In his prison writings, he was exercised by many different concerns, but one of the most important was how to speak of God, and by extension, religion, in a world of growing secularization and autonomy. Adherence to authoritative and institutional religion, as well as centuries of metaphysical conditioning and a tradition of subjective experience, would make speaking of God a difficult task:

> How do we speak of God – without religion, i.e., without the temporally conditioned presuppositions of metaphysics, inwardness, and so on? How do we speak (or perhaps we cannot now even 'speak' as we used to) in a 'secular' way about 'God'? [138]

Bonhoeffer's critique was concerned about the ways in which metaphysical concepts and the inwardness of subjectivity were aspects that shaped the religious ethos. These terms are not necessarily new to Bonhoeffer's vocabulary, but because of his reading of Wilhelm Dilthey and others he found new interpretations to deal with the idea of religion. It was Dilthey who gave to Bonhoeffer a host of ideas that allowed him to rethink the issue of religion in the midst of the growing maturation of the world.

This process of the world coming of age, whereby humankind creates a society that is self-authenticating, without recourse to the tutelage of God, is something Bonhoeffer deeply immerses himself in. It impacts his work at this time in deep and profound ways: 'Quite the contrary, in the Tegel theology Bonhoeffer is intent on addressing human beings with regard not to their sinfulness, but to their maturity. He is concerned not with the religious person (in the Barthian sense), but with the religionlessness person.'[139]

---

[137] *LPP*, p. 135.
[138] Ibid., p. 280.

In making this move to religionlessness Bonhoeffer shifts from an earlier orientation rooted in Barth and his dialectical tensions between religion and Christianity, God and humankind. He saw the world coming of age as one that will get along very well without the presuppositions of metaphysics about God, or the subjective comforts of religious projection wherein God is created in our image. This in no small measure anticipates the modern turn that calls the whole enterprise of metaphysics into question. We will take this up in fuller detail in the next chapter, but for now the age of religion is passing in Bonhoeffer's understanding because of the increasing challenges of a post-Enlightenment world. Religion cannot be protected from the critiques of the masters of suspicion when it is placed in the human *a priori*, or a metaphysical scheme that is itself historically and culturally conditioned.

In a prison letter dated 30 April 1944 Bonhoeffer writes extensively about the issue of religion and Christianity. He gives evidence of the struggle he is engaged in when he writes:

> What is bothering me incessantly is the question what Christianity really is, or indeed who Christ really is, for us today. The time when people could be told everything by means of words, whether theological or pious, is over, and so is the time of inwardness and conscience – and that means the time of religion in general. We are moving towards a completely religionless time; people as they are now simply cannot be religious any more. Even those who honestly describe themselves as 'religious' do not in the least act up to it, and so they presumably mean something quite different by 'religious'.[140]

During his imprisonment Bonhoeffer had time to reflect on the role that the Christian religion had played in shaping the citizens of Germany and he was grieved at what had been done in the name of so-called Christian civilization. How could Christianity have wrought this? It certainly had to be held responsible for the utter failure of society to resist the barbarism of Hitler and his clique, but what was the person of faith to do? How could she maintain allegiance to all that she knew to be true and still believe in Christianity? He continues this letter:

> Our whole nineteen-hundred-year-old Christian preaching and theology rest on the 'religious *a priori*', of mankind. 'Christianity' has always been a form – perhaps the true form – of 'religion'. But if one day it becomes clear that this *a priori* does not exist at all, but was a historically conditioned and transient form of

[139] Wüstenberg, p. 65.
[140] *LPP*, p. 279.

human self-expression, and if therefore man becomes radically religionless – and I think that that is already more or less the case (else how is it, for example, that this war, in contrast to all previous ones, is not calling forth any 'religious' reaction?) – what does that mean for 'Christianity'? It means that the foundation is taken away from the whole of what has up to now been our 'Christianity', and that there remain only a few 'last survivors of the age of chivalry', or a few intellectually dishonest people, on whom we can descend as 'religious'.[141]

Why is the foundation removed from Christianity? It is because Christianity had built an edifice that mirrored all the aspects of religion mentioned earlier. Its Jesus had become a politically triumphant ruler, one who had been taken captive by the entire history of Europe and beyond. It was a religion of conquistadors and inquisitors, of burning stakes and gas ovens, slaughtering those whose only sin was that the God they worshipped was different, or worse, that the other culture possessed something the religiously dominant wanted. The history of Christianity betrayed the message of the gospel and had substituted a religion ready to make any alliances with the world in order to secure its survival and dominance. It had become a religion which drew the distinctions between the pure and the impure so strongly throughout its history that it could only end up being an accomplice to the destruction of those who perished in the smoldering ashes of the Shoah.

In a manifesto published by Bonhoeffer's opponents, the German Christians, who unquestioningly supported Hitler, we find these thoughts: 'We stand on the basis of positive Christianity. Ours is an affirmative, truly national faith in Christ, in the Germanic spirit of Luther and of heroic piety,' and 'We want a Protestant church rooted in our own culture . . . We want to overcome degenerate phenomena. . . . by faith in our nation's God-given mission.'[142] Christianity in Germany had sunk to the point of utter captivity to the forces that use religion as justification for evil deeds, all done in the name of God.

For all its doctrine and history, for all its theology and philosophy, the Christian religion can function historically as just another in a long line of human creations that ultimately serve the causes of those who profit most from it. Christianity as the institutional manifestation of a living faith in the unexpected, the unforeseen, had become bankrupt. It had become religious in the worst possible way:

---

[141] Ibid., p. 280.

[142] Peter Matheson, ed., *The Third Reich and the Christian Churches* (Grand Rapids, MI: W. B. Eerdmans, 1981), pp. 4–6.

'Religious interpretation' is an exegesis of the Gospel of Christ's powerlessness that establishes priests (as the givers of life) or theologians (as the custodians of truth) as the guardians and rulers of the church's people, creating and perpetuating a situation of dependence. Nothing will be as difficult as overcoming the monarchial and patriarchal structures of hierarchies, theologies, and indeed, dogmas; coming of age contains an element that is alarmingly unreassuring.[143]

Along with this critique Bonhoeffer also returns to the matter of Christianity being more about individual salvation than doing the will of God. As mentioned earlier, this is a theme that runs throughout Bonhoeffer's theology, even though he understood by personal experience the personal appropriation of faith. He was quite critical of individualism as a category of the religious person, and when Christian faith centres itself there it runs the risk of becoming a manifestation of religious feelings and emotions. Religion is that which 'meets needs' or 'saves our souls'. For Bonhoeffer this individualism is a real danger because it removes us from the reality of what God is doing. He believed that human beings remain the focus and not God's action when we locate the saving action of God within ourselves and not the entirety of the world.[144]

In a letter dated 5 May 1944, shortly after his letter probing the dimensions of religionless Christianity, Bonhoeffer returns to this theme of the individual as a category of religion. He asks what it means to interpret Christianity and Scripture in a non-religious sense. He again returns to the categories of metaphysics and individualism as being problematic for truly understanding the biblical message and writes:

Hasn't the individualistic question about personal salvation almost completely left us all? Aren't we really under the impression that there are more important things than that question (perhaps not more important than the *matter* itself, but more important than the *question*!)?[145]

He goes on to write that the Bible is not so concerned with the individualistic doctrine of salvation, in no small part because concern with this draws our attention away from the world that God has given us to live within at the moment. By seeking escape from this life in our own salvation or piety, we deny the God who gives this life to us as a

---

[143] Bethge, p. 877.
[144] *GS* 4.202. Wüstenberg has a particularly good discussion of this, pp. 76–84.
[145] *LPP*, p. 286.

blessing. We should be attentive to this world as the place of redemption and salvation. He continues a theme that shows up early in the prison letters concerning worldliness. He indicates that when the foundation of Christianity has crumbled because its captivity to culture is done, the Christian faith is going to have to think in terms of how to define Christian belief in a worldly way. The new foundation of Christian faith, not Christian religion, will have to move the individual from concern for the world to come to concern for and immersion in this life.

This sense of worldliness will find space for itself when it does not rely on the God of religion as something that can answer all the great questions of the human heart. When we come to those moments where the great mystery of existence confounds us we often end up by referring to God as that last and ultimate space where our thinking fails us:

> Religious people speak of God when human knowledge (perhaps simply because they are too lazy to think) has come to an end, or when human resources fail – in fact it is always the *deus ex machina* that they bring on to the scene, either for the apparent solution of insoluble problems, or as strength in human failure – always that is to say, exploiting human weakness or human boundaries.[146]

Religion becomes the ultimate answer for those questions that perplex us, but this misses the mark because it too easily becomes captive to abstractions and human needs motivated more by society than God.

Bonhoeffer is writing this in the midst of the collapse not only of the German Christians, but of the Confessing Church as well. He had seen the results of what happened when in the crucible of the Nazi fire the church sought its own survival through compromise. He responds to this within a long history of moving away from the nineteenth century liberal theological tradition he was trained within, in some measure because of Barth. But as important as his intellectual musing is, it is the historical conditions that cause him to consider the passing of Christianity:

> If we don't want to do all that, if our final judgment must be that the western form of Christianity, too, was only a preliminary stage to a complete absence of religion, what kind of situation emerges for us, for the church? How can Christ become the Lord of the religionless as well? Are there religionless Christians?

---

[146] Ibid., pp. 281–82.

If religion is only a garment of Christianity – and even this garment has looked very different at different times – then what is a religionless Christianity?[147]

It is difficult for us to have the necessary perspective to understand how shaky the ground is under Bonhoeffer's feet. In one way, he is coming to grips with the entirety of his Lutheran heritage, and all that came with it. Luther's doctrine of the two kingdoms had in some measure prepared Germany for unquestioning obedience to the state as a part of God's natural order of things, and Luther's virulent anti-Semitism in the later writings of his life gave the patina of justification to the Nazi genocide. Luther had acquired the status of cultural hero in Germany and so it was an easy matter to make appeal to the trajectory of tradition that he gave to Christianity.

But it was not just the Lutheran expression of the Christian tradition that stood guilty; it was the entire religion of Christianity that had prepared the way for hatred of the Jews and their consignment into the category of the damned. Bonhoeffer saw this, though it is a question of how clearly, and realized that Christianity, as it had been mediated by history and tradition, shaped his society to accept the most heinous beliefs and practices, all in the name of God.

How can one remain a Christian and not be connected to the cultural clothing it drapes us in? This should not be just Bonhoeffer's question, it should be ours as well. How is this faith mediated to us? What are the marks and character of its adherents? How is it possible to acquire enough distance and perspective to be attentive to the voices that work to domesticate Christianity to national and cultural agendas? These questions, though framed differently weigh heavily on Bonhoeffer's mind: 'What do a church, a community, a sermon, a liturgy, a Christian life mean in a religionless world?'[148] The totality of what he understands Christianity to be is called into question and he struggles with what will rise from the ashes of Germany's collapse.

If we put too much distance between Bonhoeffer and our age then we may fail to see that these questions should burn bright for us. What has been wrought in the name of 'Christian' civilization? Our first response is usually that we do live in a 'world come of age' and that Christianity has been consigned to the domain of the individual, not the realm of national policy. Nothing in the world is done in the name of Christian society because faith has become so privatized in America.

---

[147] Ibid.
[148] Ibid., p. 280.

And yet. The 'and yet' is where it becomes subtle and tricky for us, because we are so immersed in our own worldview, so covered by our own sacred canopy, that we fail to see the ways religion is unconsciously and consciously employed to justify ourselves.

As mentioned previously, it can be as common as appealing to the just war theory, as though the wars we fight are free from political and economic agendas. Or in American society, it can be as deep as the mythology that portrays us a 'city on a hill', a nation with a 'mission', a 'light to the gentiles'. Buried deep in the heart of our national mythologies is the one that tells us that God has especially blessed us to rid the world of evil, to right the wrongs of the evildoers, and to make the world safe for democracy and freedom. This is so deeply rooted within our national psyche, so profoundly shaping of our identities and our national consciousness that we are unable to see that Bonhoeffer's critique cuts to the heart of our day as well. It is religion that provided that narrative for us.

It is not that freedom or self-determination of people is a bad thing, indeed it can be a noble goal and an admirable pursuit. In the pursuit of the freedom for others to live their lives in peace and security our nation should stand on the side of those who are oppressed and victimized. But where do we find the resources for clearly discerning when our national actions are standing on the side of the angels, as opposed to actions that are loaded with selfish and misplaced motives? How can we know when actions are undertaken that the interests of corporations and money do not fuel the engine driving events?

It is even more difficult understanding how we deceive ourselves by arguing that we are acting in the name of the good, but actually have other motives in mind. Sometimes the deception is so deep we are not even consciously aware of what our true motives are. The issue as Bonhoeffer faced it was how religion had come to so shape the national and personal identities of his nation that they were blinded to the ways in which political power used the church to further its agenda. We don't bless the destruction of others in the name of geo-political concerns. People are usually not so crass.

And yet, to do something in the name of the good, or God-given rights, or even freedom and democracy, surely that is something of which God approves? Or so we like to think. This is why Bonhoeffer speaks to us today. He helps us to understand the ways in which religion can bring out aspects of our lives that are rooted more in self and national interests than how a world might look like for those who pursue a different type of vision of life. This can be true of all peoples and all religions if the blindness to other perspectives is missing.

And, so we come to the issue of how we would know when faith has passed over into the realm of religion. Would it not be the case that the moment one says they know what the world should look like, what God requires, *absolutely*, they have fallen into the religion trap? Isn't this the problem right now? Religions all over the world claim they know what God wants with absolute certainty, and usually that is the utter eradication of the forces of darkness, the victory of light over darkness, and the destruction of the Other in the name of purity. How would we even begin to see the world with the lenses of a religionless faith? Is it possible to even take this step? Do we even want to?

This brings us back to the centrality of Jesus Christ for Bonhoeffer's faith. It is the way he understands Christ that allows him all through his life to make final appeal to Jesus as the way that saves us from the religion trap:

> The key to everything is the 'in him'. All that we may rightly expect from God and ask him for, is to be found in Jesus Christ. The God of Jesus Christ has nothing to do with what God, as we imagine him, could do and ought to do. If we are to learn what God promises, and what he fulfils, we must persevere in quiet meditation on the life, sayings, deeds, sufferings, and death of Jesus.[149]

What do we find when we do this? We don't find a system of doctrine or even right thoughts about God, but we do find God's desire to become manifest in the midst of life. Where religion separates the world into two spheres, sacred and secular, we find the God who calls us to understand it all as sacred, as sacramental, holiness incognito, which we make known through our willingness to manifest this grace. We find a living faith and not a religion that ties itself to national or ethnic identity, or psychological projections of what we wish for God to be. We find a God who is known no longer in tribal or parochial ways, but is truly universal, transcending historically conditioned boundaries. And yet here is an irony to ponder – one of the most central embodiments of this vision is in the religion of Christianity. How can it not be tainted by the forces of culture, individualism and projection? Christianity itself can never be truly pure in this sense.

Bonhoeffer throughout his life focused on how the reality of God enters the world through the incarnation found in Jesus Christ. It is

---

[149] Ibid., p. 391.

through this act that we can know what the divine intention is. But how do we guard against this historical figure becoming yet another tool in our own constructions of religion? From his earliest writings Bonhoeffer tried to grasp the dimensions of the Incarnation of God. In Barcelona, he offered a series of lectures that dealt with the role of Christ and the 'provincialism' to which Christ's teachings had succumbed. His embrace of the Sermon on the Mount in *Discipleship* and *Life Together* was an attempt to understand the uniqueness of this Christ.

In a wonderfully written section in *Ethics* Bonhoeffer takes the incarnation and fleshes out some dimensions of what he is looking for. Earlier in *Ethics* Bonhoeffer wrote that ethics is not about being good, but doing the will of God. Somewhat later we read Bonhoeffer's response to a famous biblical passage found in the Sermon on the Mount, Matthew 7:21 'Not all who say to me, " Lord, Lord, " will enter the kingdom of heaven, but only those who do the will of my Father in heaven' (Matt. 7:21). Reflecting on these words he writes:

> Thus there is a kind of confession of Christ that Jesus rejects because it is in contradiction with doing the will of God . . . Jesus will nevertheless reject this confession and doing so precisely *because* it arises out of our own human knowledge of good and evil.[150]

He goes on to say that not all confessions of Christ are actually embracing of Jesus who truly does manifest the will of God, because evil deeds can be covered with many pious words. And often it is religion that gives us the categories of good and evil without incorporating union with God as the measuring line against which life is to be discerned. And what would this union with God offer us? In a word, love, though we must be careful not to be deceived by an appeal to something that is not authentic love: 'There is a knowledge of Christ, a powerful faith in Christ, yes, even a disposition and a dedication of love unto death – all without love.'[151]

All notions of altruism, sacrifice, community, all values which we base our religion on, can be without love. Authentic love occurs within the call of God to embrace a world that is unlovable, just as Christ does. Love is able to transcend the partialities and limitations of religion, even Christianity in its religious garb. Love's essence lives on the

---

[150] *Ethics*, p. 331.
[151] Ibid., p. 332.

borders of exclusion and fear and calls for courage, hope and peace-making. Out on the frontiers of our indifference to others, it seeks the grace of reconciliation in this life, not just the world to come.

It rejoices in the truth (I Cor. 13:6.) and does not rejoice in the wrong. Often this rejoicing in the truth does not result in a thirst for the absolute, a desire to be right at another's expense, but in the creation of spaces of reconciliation and peace. It does not seek to impose on others a belief, faith or solution. It is the willingness to entertain mystery in its deepest sense. Most decidedly it is revealed to those who are Christians in the form of Jesus Christ. Bonhoeffer writes that only here do we come to know what love is. Jesus is not an abstraction, but earthly, concrete reality, borne witness to by the gospels.

This reality for the religionless Christian means that the world cannot be regarded from the boundary of religion. Religion gives us enemies and seeks to make the distinctions that divide us from one another. Christian faith, rightly understood, protects us from the temptation to hate our enemy unto death. Even worse from the perspective of those comforted by their religion, Christian faith places us closer to our enemies than we wish to be:

> Jesus Christ, however, was in the midst of his enemies. It was precisely there that he wanted to be. And there we, too, should be. That distinguishes us from all other teachers and religions. The devout want to be among themselves. Christ, however, wants us to be in the midst or our enemies, just as he was.[152]

One of the reasons that religion is ultimately incapable of love for one's own enemy is because it does not want its enemy to have a faith other than its own. Often in the religious mind there can only be one way to the life of God. Religion marks the territory where we exclude and exile. It makes no space for the Other. Through the power of its myths and narratives it places us in the world to define ourselves to the harm of others. Sure, we are supposed to love, but to love the unbeliever, the infidel? To be in the midst of our enemies means that we are willing to see them and their lives with the same compassion that Jesus possesses.

The religion that Bonhoeffer was seeking to deconstruct is the habit of heart that allows us to approach the world without love, even while declaring that we are doing just the opposite. But the religionless Christian does not seek to protect her own space at the expense of

---

[152] *GS* 4:431. Würstenburg, p. 13.

others, or distort the truth to fit her culturally induced notion of who is in and who is out. Authentic faith, Bonhoeffer writes, causes us to place ourselves in the midst of our enemies, not seeking to destroy them, but to bring reconciliation to them as God has brought reconciliation to us. Religionless Christianity is life lived for others without claiming cultural or spiritual privilege.

But does this not place us in an untenable position? Are we not back to the issue that those who take seriously the radical demands of Jesus are caught between historical necessity and the ethic of Jesus? How does the follower of Jesus become responsible to the world as it is? If we follow Bonhoeffer's ideas we are supposed to be immersed within the world. We cannot ignore the reality of the world by some all too easy call to 'love one another'. Does not the love of another mean the protection of them from harm? If love is the best that religionless Christianity can do, then maybe we are better off with the justice of religion.

We will fill out the dimensions of this later on as we examine Bonhoeffer's move to the conspiracy, however, for now a few ideas of what religionless faith might look like.[153] Love recognizes that truth does not come in stories that will the death of my brother and sister in the name of God, or the idols of secularity, security and wealth. The willingness to walk in the steps of the Crucified means a desire to create the space for those whose religion is different, whose identity is different, wherever we may be on the planet. These spaces will be the spaces of peacemaking and reconciliation.

> Inscribed on the very heart of God's grace is the rule that we can be its recipients only if we do not resist being made into its agents; what happens to us must be done by us. Having been embraced by God, we must make space for others in ourselves and invite them in – even our enemies.[154]

This is not a cheap grace, it is a costly grace. We fear the religionless faith because it makes us vulnerable in the world the way God is vulnerable in the world and who is like unto God? But the character of faith

---

[153] The ideas that follow in no way are Bonhoeffer's own, however, if we follow the trajectory of his thinking into our own time the issue of relationship among the religious communities stands strong on the concerns that must be engaged by Christians. Of particular concern is the tension to remain faithful to the revelation of God in Jesus Christ while welcoming those who do not share that faith into an embrace that does not demand conversion.

[154] Volf, 129.

is found in the lived character of its adherents and if we wish merely to ape the world and employ our gods to fight for us then let us not cling to the fiction that we are following Jesus Christ. For nowhere does Jesus allow for the legitimizing of political gains by violence. Christian religion may allow for this, but Jesus does not. This is the reality of a faith without religion that Bonhoeffer struggled with so throughout his life. We turn now to thinking about the ways in which religionless Christianity takes shape in the world.

Chapter 5

ONLY THE SUFFERING GOD CAN HELP

In her book, *The Silent Cry: Mysticism and Resistance*, the theologian Dorothee Soelle relates the story of a conference she attended where the question was raised: 'Where was God at Auschwitz?' One of those attending the conference session responded by asserting that Auschwitz was willed by God. Pressed further about this statement she responded that if God had not willed it, it would not have happened. Nothing happens without God willing it to be so, she argued. Soelle calls this God the idol.[155]

This is the world of religion; the desire to control the world through our images of God finds a home here. How God gets defined significantly impacts the religious dimension because the term God itself signifies everything we believe to be the absolute. We invest this term with words such as omniscience, omnipotence and omnipresence, but these terms become essentially meaningless in the realm of concrete reality. They function instead as religious categories we use in an attempt to control God, thinking, of course, that we are doing the exact opposite.

This is always the problem with theology, however, because it too often becomes the unknowing attempt to manage something that is essentially uncontrollable by us. When Bonhoeffer is writing he has his mind very distinctly on the critique of religion that those like Nietzsche and Feuerbach offered. In these levelling critiques we are met with the challenge that powerful clerical and ecclesial interests conspire to keep people imprisoned in illusion and deception by the use of language. We use language in such a way that the interpretations are

---

[155] Dorothee Soelle, *The Silent Cry: Mysticism and Resistance*, trans. Barbara and Martin Rumscheidt (Minneapolis, MN: Fortress Press, 2001), p. 110.

controlled by those who establish what the words convey. We have no firm grasp on reality; all we have are interpretations, the authority of which rests with those who construct the interpretations. Nietzsche is relentless in his attack on all forms of religion that claim to know the truth, when it is really power they are after.

For those who take this critique to heart, all claims to truth must be abandoned and understood as claims to power disguised in the cloak of self and corporate deception. And this is true not just for religion, but for every human inquiry into knowledge. This is just one manifestation of humankind's movement to autonomy in the 'world come of age'. All things now stand under the umbrella of critique since nothing can be assumed to be true because of appeals to communal assumptions about reality.

One path taken in the new world was marked out by Schleiermacher who sought the explication of religious beliefs as interpretations of religious experience. When religious beliefs and traditions became grounded in the religious (or Christian) self-consciousness, the authority for revelation shifted from the external ground of texts and tradition to the interior realms of human subjectivity. Standing at the end of this path, though, were those who pointed out that the human subject was as helpless as traditional or textual authority to provide any foundational certainty that would be free of human limitation. And, as always, Nietzsche was there to remind us that the human subject not only manipulated and did violence to others in the name of truth self-constructed, but we are so self-deluded that we sincerely believe our own constructions to be the truth.

When we look back at the thousands of years that have been spent in constructing our images of God we find, according to this critique, that all our attempts at talking about God have actually been exercises in talking about ourselves instead. Bonhoeffer grasped this with fresh urgency from his prison cell. As we saw earlier, Bonhoeffer knew that the world of institutional and authoritative religion would make speaking a true word about God a difficult task.

He wondered how religious language can say a true word about God. He knew that the cultural–religious manifestations of Christianity in particular used religion as a cloak for projects having nothing to do with faith. Where could we find the authentic presence of God in the midst of words that were used to distort and twist truth? How could we use language to express the reality of God in a world that was not the projection of our own desires and wishes? These were questions that Bonhoeffer was asking.

Bonhoeffer's analysis of religion addressed the fact that those anxious souls who used the religion of Christianity in its transcendental clothing to answer questions about the unknown dimensions of life and death constructed a religious idol. What may be difficult for us to realize is that the entirety of the Christian tradition may be captured by this idolatry. There is a whole stream of theology which has used God as the stop-gap, the *deus ex machina*, to fill in the gaps of human knowing.

Concerning God, the terms we have used to define the Divine like omnipotence or omniscience are in fact theological mistakes that say something about our relationship to power or our relationship to knowledge. We have constructed a metaphysics that is reflective of our extending concepts familiar to us into the realm of the transcendent and making those concepts an absolute that we then project onto God. When religiously based metaphysics of being was used in this way it resulted in a God taken captive by our language.

This type of spatial transcendence corresponded to the mythological constructs of religion that constructed God in their image. Bonhoeffer argues that 'God's "beyond" is not the beyond of our cognitive faculties. The transcendence of epistemological theory has nothing to do with the transcendence of God. God is beyond in the midst of our life.'[156] An innate connection between thought and being was one that Bonhoeffer believed delivered God over into our hands.

A metaphysical approach that wraps God in a culturally conditioned notion of Being objectifies God in the dimensions of a particular age and within religion acquires a status of absolute truth, impervious from question. This is the religious idol, made from the storehouse of our own construction, though we remain unaware of our productive role in this. Religious language can be one of the greatest barriers against the reality of God:

> Supranatural and mythological formulations obscure the Gospel's direct immediacy, and the exotic nature of the context in which it is presented has nothing to do with the message itself. Instead of this, however, the metaphysically organized Christian religion provided the world with the kind of transcendence that it longed for. God became necessary as the superstructure of being, and religious longing found its goal in a heavenly domain. Thus metaphysics seduces the Christian religion into thinking statically in terms of two spheres and has forced it to give its redemptive nature a one-sided emphasis.[157]

[156] *LPP*, p. 282.

Bonhoeffer knew that a category such as God's omnipotence was not to be seen as an authentic aspect of God's nature, but was our understanding of power extended out into the world. But once we know that this is the case what do we do with the fact that theism itself may be weighted with this burden? For one thing, we could recognize that foundational certainty in theology is more difficult than we might have imagined. There is no neutral, objective, secure position that protects theology from the cultural or linguistic limitations of humankind. Nothing protects Christianity from the erosions of a 'world come of age'.

The awareness of the interpretive and historical character of theology has become especially acute as we become alert to the interconnections between knowledge and power. The critiques of dissenting theologies reveal the suspicion that metaphysics and inward experience cannot offer universal foundations for talking about God. It is precisely the place where universal grounds are argued that should raise the greatest question because those are the claims that are most inherently manipulative over the consciences of human beings. More often we are taking contingent historical aspects of human existence and claiming universal authority of notions of God that are partial and limited.

In the 'world come of age' God is not a reality which is a given and constitutive part of our consciousness, and speech about or to God can never be presupposed to be directly referential. We bring to the task of interpreting our lives a host of background assumptions and presuppositions that form the web of understanding. For the critic this raises the question of how theology can be anything other than a self-deluded attempt to wield power and define reality for those who want theologians to do their thinking for them? Does every age's construal of God lose force when the experiences and language of that age fade into the coming one, reflecting the self and corporate interests of the newest order? Is this not the dilemma of religious language? It is the attempt to reach the transcendent, but it can claim no space protected from the vagaries of history. This takes us into the heart of Bonhoeffer's critique of religion.

---

[157] Bethge, p. 873. There is a question as to whether metaphysics is unavoidable. Even if we disregard Hellenist ideas we will still have Hegel or any other scheme of interpretation for the processes of life and history.

If our most cherished space of religion is understood as the creation of humans shaped by traditions, language, belief systems and rituals, conditioned by historical contingency, how are we to create paradigms or establish priorities in the face of shifting contexts? Are we left to the realization that all theological strategies are self-generated and illusionary? We stand in the room of historical consciousness and wonder how to contend for interpretations of life that reveal something other than the current assumptions of contemporary concerns. Where do we find something other than our own projective identifications?

Or maybe it is worse than this because we may be led to the truth of Nietzsche that there is no God in history or in nature, but what we experience and revere as God is miserable, absurd, a crime against life. The God of religion may indeed represent a flight from the world and its struggles to the illusion of another world. The type of God created by Nietzsche's 'slave mentality' serves the need of human illusion and self-deification by self-crucifixion and self-violation. By this type of self-sacrifice, the human is able to establish harmony with the One-All. Religious language has conspired to legitimate the weak, delusional and self-crucifying illusions we call God.

Bonhoeffer understood this and he writes insightfully from his cell about just this tendency in Christianity. He, too, is wondering what is essential, decisive and normative to faith. He stood in a situation where Christianity took many different forms, most of them reflective of the very difficulties just mentioned. Christianity as he had experienced it most recently was an expression of power and a domain of influence meant to manipulate and deceive persons. Bonhoeffer was trying to develop a way of response to this profanation. His distrust for the category of religion was rooted in the belief that religion can reflect a flight from reality and a refusal to resist those who cause so much destruction in earthly existence. In the face of atrocity where does religion offer something other than legitimation of the powers?

In the intersection between humankind's search for meaning and its religious symbols there does exist a space that marks it as a candidate for our consideration though. This space is marked by the concreteness that marked Bonhoeffer's own theology. He was strongly opposed to abstractions being used as a substitute for involvement in the world. This concreteness was always rooted christologically: Jesus Christ is where God becomes concrete reality, original reality. Transcendence is removed from metaphysical speculation and related to life in all its manifestations through embodiment.

And in this life, we find one constant aspect that transcends historical contingency or metaphysical speculation – suffering. As a fundamental aspect of human life, it is transhistorical and immediate.
Suffering brings us to the door of human being and cuts across the
ideological, social and economic categories we use to interpret and
shape our existence. Suffering stands as a critique to the 'world come
of age'. Those who suffer present themselves before all our accom-
plishments and offer mute testimony to the power claimed by our
technology, science and politics. These shadows emerge from the mists
of our indifference with names on their lips that haunt us, Hiroshima,
Auschwitz, Rwanda, Darfur, Iraq. How does God language respond to
this? How does religion respond? When Bonhoeffer interrogates religion and, by extension, theology, he raises questions that reveal the
unspoken social and political agendas found in any cultural context
where theology is done.

When theology fails to ask the question of who benefits most from a
particular theological perspective and silently offers justifications for
the reigning order, it manifests the difference between the religious
and nonreligious interpretations of Christian faith. A religious interpretation springs from the will to power that rests comfortably with the
suffering of others in the name of some larger cause. The nonreligious
call of Christianity is a call to create a community whose members exist
in a distinct relationship to the world. This community is formed from
the understanding that theologies reflective of power are overturned
by the God who suffers. As we saw before, Bonhoffer argued that only
the suffering God could help:

> The Bible directs man to God's powerlessness and suffering; only the suffering
> God can help. To that extent we may say the development towards the world
> coming of age outlined above, which has done away with a false conception of
> God, opens up a way of seeing the God of the Bible who wins power and space in
> the world by his weakness. This will probably be the starting point of our 'secular
> interpretation.'[158]

If we ask who benefits from Bonhoeffer's theology, we find that
the incarnate presence of God in Christ makes Bonhoeffer sensitive
to the universality of suffering. This grasp of human suffering conditions religionless Christianity to embody solidarity with the powerless.

---

[158] *LPP*, p. 361.

Religionless Christianity does not seek out the powerful, rather it responds to the suffering created by those who wield power in the world. And in this response we find something different than a theology that defines God in terms of power. The theology of glory moves to the theology of the cross.[159] The possibility of a nonreligious interpretation emerges from a different space altogether, a space that calls forth from us a different relationship to God. In the section of prison writings entitled 'Outline for a Book', Bonhoeffer reflects on how this might take shape:

> Who is God? Not in the first place an abstract belief in God, in his omnipotence, etc. That is not a genuine experience of God, but a partial extension of the world. Encounter with Jesus Christ. The experience that a transformation of all human life is given in the fact that 'Jesus is there for others'. His 'being there for others' is the experience of transcendence. . . . Faith is participation in this being of Jesus (incarnation, cross, and resurrection). Our relation to God is not a 'religious' relationship to the highest, most powerful, and best Being imaginable –that is not authentic transcendence – but our relation to God is a new life in 'existence for others,' through participation in the being of Jesus. The transcendental is not infinite and unattainable tasks, but the neighbour who is within reach in any given situation.[160]

Religion constructs for us certain responses to the universal aspect of suffering. In the myths of redemption some power is at work to restore the broken relationship between God and the world that will be made manifest in the next life, when the shards of light within us are able to reunite with the light of the next world. Or, perhaps, salvation will come with a restoration of unity, with harmony of the One-All that constitutes a totalizing unity with itself. It might even come with the omnipotent God finally taking the power of the absolute and asserting all power on earth.[161] Ultimately the suffering find their relief on the other side of the veil.

Bonhoeffer sees Christianity standing in a somewhat different space because in response to the suffering of the world he does not envision

---

[159] Bonhoeffer was prepared for this in no small part from his Lutheran tradition. Luther employs these terms significantly throughout his theology.

[160] *LPP*, p. 381.

[161] Of course, Christianity itself is not immune from these images. In its apocalyptic images, the images of the rider on the white horse in Revelation will execute justice. But read from the position of those who have lived lives of oppression at the hands of the powerful, Revelation looks very much different from those who have lived in the centres of power and interpreted Christian faith accordingly.

the reality of God being made manifest in the religious constructions of life in a world to come, but in the willingness of the disciple to follow a different vision. The life of God in the world is not to be defined in terms that make God's reality so radically transcendent that the horizons between God and humankind are merely tangential, barely connecting with one another.[162] Religious impulses might seek God in the ultimate reality of the great beyond, but religionless Christianity seeks the life of God immersed in the world of everyday life and the suffering of those who participate in it.

For Bonhoeffer, empirical reality shapes the authentic dimensions of a nonreligious faith. Theology can devise conceptual schemes of transcendence or other metaphysical categories; but, for Bonhoeffer, faith in the end is a lived moment. The constellation of his thought oscillates around life in the here and now, not in the beyond:

> I discovered later, and I'm still discovering right up to this moment, that it is only by living completely in this world that one learns to have faith . . . By this worldliness I mean living unreservedly in life's duties, problems, successes, and failures, . . . experiences and perplexities. In so doing, we throw ourselves completely into the arms of God, taking seriously not only our own sufferings, but those of God in the world – watching with Christ in Gethsemane.[163]

STRUGGLING IN THE GARDEN

How does one watch with Christ in Gethsemane however? Bonhoeffer had different ideas about this throughout his life and this creates the grounds from which so many different interpretations of him arise. When he is writing *Discipleship* he infuses it with ideas about suffering, but it is suffering being-for-others that stands at a distance from the world. It is a suffering that leads one to a hermetically sealed space that moves through the world on its way to its heavenly destination, 'The church-community moves through the world like a sealed train

---

[162] See, for example, Karl Barth's early statement in *The Epistle to the Romans* about this horizon, trans. Edwyn C. Hoskyns (London: Oxford University Press, 1980), p. 10; pp. 29–31.

[163] Ibid., pp. 369–70. In some ways this is expressed elsewhere as Bonhoeffer makes continual reference to the life revealed in the Jewish Scriptures. The narratives expressed in the stories of the patriarchs and prophets show persons not so much concerned with a life after this one, but people so immersed in this life the next one is not even thought about.

passing through foreign territory.'[164] While the church is visible, it nonetheless stands at a vast distance from the world and serves as the alternative community of worship that 'invades the world and snatches its children.'[165]

In *Ethics* and *Letters and Papers from Prison* Bonhoeffer nuances this in favour of understanding something very different about how suffering becomes the path of Christian life. It is not a suffering that exists in isolation from the responsibilities of life, but one that takes us into the centre of the suffering of the world:

> The Christian, unlike the devotees of the redemption myths, has no last line of escape available from earthly tasks and difficulties into the eternal, but, like Christ himself ('My God, why hast thou forsaken me?') he must drink the earthly cup to the dregs, and only in his doing so is the crucified and risen Lord with him, and he crucified and risen with Christ. This world must not be prematurely written off; in this the Old and New Testaments are at one. Redemption myths arise from human boundary-experiences, but Christ takes hold of a man at the centre of his life.[166]

Religious interpretation uses the afterlife or some heavenly goal as the ultimate end and thus the penultimate becomes sacrificed on the altar of the ultimate. The embodiment of God found in the Incarnation of Christ sets the stage for all critiques of religion used in this way. This escape into another life is the last place that a religionless Christianity concerns itself with, rather it is the very earthy being of Jesus that is of primary concern:

> God in human form – not, as in oriental religions, in animal form, monstrous, chaotic, remote, terrifying, nor in the conceptual forms of the absolute, metaphysical, infinite, etc. nor yet in the Greek divine-human form of 'man in himself'; but the 'man for others' and therefore the Crucified, the man who lives out of the transcendent.[167]

Ultimately the embrace of a religionless Christianity takes us to a place of suffering the cross, but not to escape the world in individual piety or otherworldly mysticism. Rather we call the world into question by our very immersion and being in the world, sharing its duties, sorrows and sufferings. This is where the work of love becomes gritty

---

[164] *Discipleship*, p. 260.
[165] Ibid., p. 233.
[166] *LPP*, p. 337.
[167] Ibid., pp. 381–82.

and life threatening. This is why the church has no protected space, no true separation from the world.

A religionless Christianity takes the responsibility to confront the world with a challenging word, but to its own surprise this is not the word of dominance, or power, exemplified by the rule of the righteous. This vision of the life of God, rooted in God's suffering, creates an inherent instability in the world because it is not built upon the ideologies of nation–states or other forces like religion that drive so much of the world presently. It is the reality of the suffering God, found in Christ, who himself is immersed continually in the world. For Bonhoeffer after Finkenwalde, the life of God is no longer found just in the church, it is embedded within the life of the world which suffers.

This suffering, viewed theologically, constitutes space for reflection on the Incarnation. For it is in Christ that in some mysterious way God is abandoned in the world. Categories of theological abstraction such as omnipotence suffer the cross as well because they become the boundary limits that define the reality of God for many in the tradition. And this in turn leads us to such a distance from God that we try and use various means for restoring the relationship.

One way the religious path takes shape in fleeing suffering is the desire to escape our bodies, or at the very least to try and put off our natural/sinful self. We use purification rituals or sacrificial performance when in truth we are enfolded within the life of God even in our felt abandonment. It is in the absence of God that I reach the end of my religious belonging and can stand by God in God's own hour of suffering. I find God *'When I, a human being, experience myself as cut off from God, at that very moment of the utmost abjection, I am absolutely close to God, since I find myself in the position of the abandoned Christ.'*[168] We find here echoes of Bonhoeffer's existence in prison. We stand by God in God's own hour of suffering, but God continually suffers within and at the hands of the world that God created.

STANDING WITH THE SUFFERING

The sensitivity to suffering marked Bonhoeffer's life and it shows up throughout his life. It is not a new or novel idea that our participation in the being of Jesus means we find ourselves immersed within the

---

[168] Slavoj Žižek, *On Belief* (London: Routledge, 2001), p. 146.

sufferings of the world. Bonhoeffer had other ideas about this in the book *Discipleship.* One of the central concerns he had in this writing was the place of the Sermon on the Mount. At that point his life had taken on its specific mission in confrontation with the National Socialist regime that racked Germany. While he may have been somewhat isolated in Finkenwalde, he had his finger on the pulse of the nation in many ways. When he writes he is under no illusion about the evil that he is facing.

He starts the section on the Sermon on the Mount by pointing out that Luther emphasized the bearing of suffering as a part of Christian life. Bonhoeffer goes on to state that it is this bearing that marks Jesus' suffering on the cross, but it is also a mark of those who follow Jesus that they will also suffer.[169] And, why do they suffer? They do so because they ' . . . *renounce violence and strife.* Those things never help the cause of Christ.'[170]

This cause of Christ is borne by the faith community formed in his name. This constitutes a new type of community, a distinctly visible community that is meant to serve as an alternative polis to the world within which Christians find themselves. The desire to flee into invisibility is to deny Christ's call. An invisible community that seeks to disappear into its piety in order to be humble becomes a community turned in on itself and thus in some regard becomes a religious community because it flees from the suffering of others. To bear suffering does not mean acquiescence to the oppressor, it means to respond to evil in a way that does not allow for self-justification by those who act evilly.

The community which seeks to make itself visible in the world will of necessity be a community of resistance, not because it desires enmity with the world, but because 'Jesus' community ought to examine whether it has given a sign of Jesus' love, which preserves, supports, and protects lives, to those whom the world has despised and dishonored.'[171] Against all those orders of the state that categorized the worth of persons on what they could contribute to the regime, or what they were able to produce for the militaristic aims of Germany, Bonhoeffer believed that Christian faith should not view persons by the lens of their utilitarian usefulness to the culture. Human lives should not be

[169] *Discipleship,* p. 107.
[170] Ibid., p. 108.
[171] Ibid., p. 123.

shoved into a collective that pursues goals and ends that are at enmity with God's intention for life revealed in Christ.

Elsewhere Bonhoeffer writes: 'There is no worthless life before God, because God holds life itself to be valuable.'[172] Because of their value to God persons are not to be seen as means to an end. One of the initial moves to understand the compassion of God comes from a clear recognition of the sufferings of others. Contempt for this type of compassion will shape and form a person in certain ways that leads away from the life that God desires for the creation.[173] But the visible community of Christ is called to stand with the suffering because it is called to be the community of reconciliation and healing. Because of this commitment the faithful have other commitments that relativize all other allegiances. All political and social allegiances are provisional: 'For Christians there is no such thing as absolute earthly allegiance. A loyalty oath which intends to bind a Christian absolutely is a lie that comes from "the evil one."'[174]

This belief alone establishes those who embrace something other than country, nation or state as worthy of ultimate allegiance to be threats to those who wield power. It may mean that other grounds for the moral legitimacy of actions exist that are not controlled by the state. It may also imply that the actions of the nation or other communities that forces events into situations where the suffering and destruction of others occurs are inherently ungodly and even evil. Certainly those who lived in Bonhoeffer's day were able to offer ample justifications for the course their nation took, but it is to the shame of the Christian church that they were unable to offer something other than the feeblest of voices when the destructive seeds that lay behind the Nazi collective began sprouting their toxic and noxious fruit of death.

---

[172] *Ethics*, p. 193.

[173] This leads Bonhoeffer to write in *Ethics* about the protection of life in all its forms, especially the most vulnerable, but the impetus for this comes in no small measure from the realization that God is present in these who are suffering and it is only here where we stand with God in God's hour of suffering. In these sections, Bonhoeffer specifically lists those the Nazi regime had targeted for extinction.

[174] *Discipleship*, p. 130. This is striking language because it shows what type of resistance the community of Christ calls for. On 9 August 1934 Ludwig Müller had led the German Evangelical National Synod to pass a requirement for all pastors and church officials to swear a loyalty oath saying they would be 'faithful and obedient to the *Führer* of the German people and state, Adolf Hitler.' This might also give one pause when considering what pledges of allegiance they are asked to make in our day.

The form of this resistance to that which seeks to destroy the life of God in the world Bonhoeffer found in the Sermon on the Mount, but the shape of this had surprising consequences. Dealing with the law of retribution he shows that Jesus relativizes the law in such a way that the community of Israel is released from political and legal orders, not bound by political or national ties. They are bound to a new order, an order rooted in something different even than previous religious belief.

This order meant that 'Assault is condemned by not being met with violence.'[175] The only way evil can come to an end and suffering stop is when we are willing to suffer in bearing it by not taking the way of violence:

> Our voluntary renunciation of counterviolence confirms and proclaims our unconditional allegiance to Jesus as his followers, our freedom, our detachment from our own egos. And it is only in the exclusivity of this adherence that evil can be overcome.[176]

The suffering of the disciple is the suffering of one who suffers the cross of bearing wrong, even evil, for the sake of the world: 'The more terrible the evil, the more willing the disciple should be to suffer.'[177] Bonhoeffer considers this aspect of suffering to be crucial for his understanding of how the community of faith responds to suffering. One reason this is so is because it gives the enemy no excuses or justifications for those who use violence to destroy their enemy. In standing fast this way, the person of faith does not allow the moral chaos of their opponent to suck them into the vortex of their own self-justifying madness. Bonhoeffer offers this as the authentic Christian response to evil, and does so from within the belly of the Nazi beast.

The question that immediately comes to mind is whether or not Bonhoeffer is being completely naïve? Does he not recognize at this point in time the danger that the Nazis present? Can we take this message to heart as anything other than the pious platitudes of someone who is deluded and captive to the slave mentality Nietzsche so despises? Does Bonhoeffer not recognize that we have enemies who want to kill us? Bonhoeffer was not unaware of this. He knew in fact that the

---

[175] Ibid., 133.
[176] Ibid.
[177] Ibid., 134.

community of faith had many enemies in Nazi Germany. These forces wanted nothing less than the eradication of all those who opposed them. He gives a whole section of *Discipleship* just to the issue of the enemy and in fact understands quite clearly the historical situation he is in. He writes: '*The time of a widespread persecution of Christians is coming*, and that is actually the real meaning of all the movements and struggles of our time.'[178] He goes on to write that resistance to this persecution will have to take place within a community which worships and prays.

He continues to write that the community of faith responds to the enemy in such a way a space opens for a new and different way of being in the world. The enemy who wishes our destruction is one whose wounds and pain are great, whose neediness and poverty, guilt and estrangement from God and humankind are great. If it were otherwise they would not be our enemy. The question may be posed, why is this person my enemy and where does suffering emerge to call me to the cross of my putting away my own self-protection in order to make space for the enemy Other?

This truly does take us into suffering Gethsemane for these questions take us into difficult territory. Does Christ really call us to bear the sufferings of our enemy? Would this not mean an attempt to grasp what those sufferings consist of? How does this happen if my desire for self-protection trumps the willingness to suffer interrogation by the sufferings of the enemy Other? How, in fact, did this person become my enemy? If my enemy is seeking my death does my unwillingness to kill him first not imply willing acquiescence to evil?

In the theological milieu that Bonhoeffer lived within, the Christian religion was conceptualized in such a way that God became the One who causes all things in life to be exactly what they already are. This echoes the conference attendee who said that nothing happens without God willing it to be so. Even in the 'world come of age' religion establishes the orders under which many live their lives. These orders tell me that God establishes my very core identity. The order of religion defines me in the world, it tells me who I am and to defy these orders is to put myself outside the will of God. These orders exist within

---

[178] *Discipleship*, p. 142. Putting aside for a minute the fact that Bonhoeffer's vision frames the struggles which engaged him as ultimately about the church, he still understands that the type of faith that offers its ultimate allegiance to God is one that the world will have to destroy. At the deepest level, the world and God remain estranged.

nation, family, country, even religion. Anything that touches the preservation of these things is by definition my enemy.[179]

As mentioned previously, these are the ways that we have constructed
the world and much of the strife and violence that plague the earth
have been in no small part because of real or perceived threats to the
borders that we have erected that are ephemeral and transitory. Jesus
relativizes these orders as well. Inasmuch as religion has been an aspect
of this it has constructed idols that mask the true nature of reality and
keep us unaware or unconcerned about the suffering we cause in the
world. The gods, it would seem, have been employed to keep us in
communities of separation and finitude to serve the needs of those
who desire to control.

It would appear even further that religion creates the gods to satisfy
our need for something universal to worship. This desire for universality can also serve to close us off from the sufferings of others. Fyodor
Dostoyevsky, writing in his novel *The Brothers Karamozov*, understood
how the religious dimension shapes us in such a way that the gods
serve our fears rather than our hopes. Religion creates the totalitarian
God who becomes the great necessity everyone must agree to and bow
down before. And it will destroy all those who refuse to bend the knee
to it:

> This craving for community of worship is the chief misery of every man individu-
> ally and of all humanity from the beginning of time. For the sake of common
> worship they have slain each other with the sword. They have set up gods and
> challenged one another, 'Put away your gods and come and worship ours, or we
> will kill you and your gods!' And so it will be to the end of the world, even when
> gods disappear from the earth; they will fall down before idols just the same.[180]

The boundaries we create out of historical contingency function as
the engines of violence because what we create, we protect, even unto
death. As much role as the market and the ideologies of nation–states
factor into construction of communities of conflict, religion serves its
role as well to create enemies and mask their suffering from us in order

---

[179] This was one of the biggest theological struggles that was taking place in
Germany at this time. On the one side were those theologians who were arguing precisely that the orders that existed did so because of God's will. Bonhoeffer rejected
talk of orders in favour of other language. At the end of his life he is using the term
'mandates' to speak to the way in which God's governance of the world operates.

[180] Fyodor Dostoyevsky, *The Brothers Karamozov*, trans. David McDuff (New York, NY:
Penguin Press, 1993), p. 296.

that we may not truly recognize our participation in the destruction of other lives.

In Bonhoeffer's writings from Finkenwalde, especially in his grasp of suffering, we find the hope for a community created in faithfulness to Jesus as a sign of radical resistance to these conflicting orders because the disciple's lives are not determined by the boundaries of nation, state, blood or soil. This community is not even formed from religious impulses that result in more separation and violence. This community is formed by God in Christ who calls us to a new order of life in the world, an order that loves fiercely that which God creates, even the enemy.

This willingness to love the enemy constitutes the greatest threat to the powers today because they simply cannot control this manifestation of God's grace. The willingness to suffer the enemy, to hear them, to feel the anguish when their children die, to grieve when their families are destroyed, the desire to reconcile and heal in the midst of so much anger and hatred, these things are absolutely foreign to the ideologies which drive the 'world come of age'. This suffering with the enemy brings us to the heart of reversal that heralds the life of God made manifest in the midst of the realities that we create.

As Bonhoeffer warns though, this is not done without a great deal of suffering on our part. It is only when the suffering of others becomes my own suffering that I can stand as a force for God's way in the world revealed in Jesus Christ:

> How does love become unconquerable? By never asking what the enemy is doing to it, and only asking what Jesus has done. Loving one's enemies leads disciples to the way of the cross and into communion with the crucified one.[181]

As long as one stays connected to certain realities, established and maintained by the culture or society one is shaped by, one's enemies on a large scale are likely to be chosen by the community you find yourself within. There will always be those who will be able to find ample evidence of the harm done to your way of life by the enemy because the cycles of violence have been embedded in your interactions with those others. In exactly this way the 'world come of age' allows the spirit of destruction to define it. Those forces of culture that seek compliance to the constructions of nation or state are difficult to resist, especially when so much energy is exerted to maintain the

---

[181] *Discipleship*, p. 141.

narratives they use to control us. Bonhoeffer's particular discernment existed in his ability to detach from the orders that sought to define him, thus acquiring the freedom to contend for other ways of being in the world.

In so far as many in Germany were contending on theological grounds for obedience to the state and the destruction of the state's enemies in the name of God, their theology is reflective of all the worst aspects mentioned earlier in this chapter. The realization that their theology was justifying massive suffering and oppression, even to the point of genocide, was absolutely hidden from them. What causes this type of blindness in the face of such evil should give us pause for no one in our time is immune from this level of self and corporate deception.

Religionless Christianity becomes a threat to the powers that seek control because it does not succumb to appeals for community or solidarity on the basis of hatred or fear of the enemy. The emergence of the community of Christ as Bonhoeffer envisioned it his entire life should lead to the formation of something new in the world, something foreign to the arrangements that the world has made for itself. Its compassion should be rooted in something other than transitory allegiances to provisionary appeals to unity.

A compassion that is based in Christ's sufferings responds to others without regard to historical contingencies and in doing so disrupts and disturbs the worlds we create because this response to suffering becomes profoundly subversive. While ideology is busy constructing boundaries to keep us at one another's throats, love works another part of the bullet-ridden streets:

> As every true Christian knows, love is the *work* of love – the hard and arduous work of repeated 'uncoupling' in which, again and again, we have to disengage ourselves from the inertia that constrains us to identify with the particular order we were born into.[182]

Dietrich Bonhoeffer knew this well enough in his life. He knew that he could no longer view the world through the lenses of his comfortable bourgeois background. He knew this because of a lifetime of experiences that led him to many other parts of the world, where he saw the

---

[182] Slavoj Žižek, *The Fragile Absolute or, Why is the Christian Legacy Worth Fighting for?* (London and New York: Verso, 2000), p. 128.

sufferings of others. He also knew it from the crucible of the fire that consumed him. In a well-known piece written to his friends and those in the conspiracy, he writes that he learned to see the events of history 'from the perspective of the outcast, the suspects, the maltreated, the powerless, the oppressed, the reviled – in short, from the perspective of those who suffer.'[183]

This grasp of suffering puts Bonhoeffer far from understanding God in any way that makes theology referential to metaphysics or inward subjectivity as the primary categories with which to understand or grapple with the reality of the divine. The remoteness of the God of metaphysics leads us far away from the reality of God's life as Bonhoeffer understood it. But the movement away from theological tradition was accompanied by a sensitivity to suffering that calls all theology into question if it does not respond to the destruction the world visits upon those who are 'the outcasts, the suspects, the maltreated, the powerless, the oppressed, the reviled.'

When one looks at life from the perspective of those at the mercy of the great powers and notices the structures in place which abuse and oppress those who suffer, the result can be disorienting. Seen clearly, the idea of 'business as usual' and 'this is just the way the world is' seems problematic. This is one reason why Bonhoeffer resonated so strongly with the theologians of liberation. He grasped that the way we respond to suffering corresponds in no small measure to the ways that we define God. If we see in the sufferings of the world the reality that God is suffering, it becomes more difficult to participate in or justify that which causes more suffering.

Bonhoeffer carried suffering as a primary theological concern far beyond his time at Finkenwalde. He writes powerfully of the impact of suffering in *Ethics* as well. Here the willing acceptance of suffering may lead to hatred, humiliation and guilt incurred by Jesus Christ. This suffering rests as well in the heart of the cross for Christ, and for us, in vulnerability to the world. In a section dealing with, 'Ethics as Formation' Bonhoeffer writes:

> This love of God for the world does not withdraw from reality into noble souls detached from the world, but experiences and suffers the reality of the world at its worst. The world exhausts its rage on the body of Jesus Christ.[184]

---

[183] *LPP*, p. 17.
[184] *Ethics*, p. 83.

In the midst of moral struggle about participation in the conspiracy Bonhoeffer is wrestling with the ways that Christ takes form in the world and the ways we are formed to be the manifestation of Christ. He tries to differentiate the ways in which the church can manifest something other than religious concerns: 'The church's concern is not religion, but the form of Christ and its taking form among a band of people.'[185] The form of Christ in the world is not found among the political powers or the wealthy, rather it is found among the powerless and suffering of society, which are themselves the space of Christ's presence in the world. Here is where God is present, hidden from sight, incognito, *deus absconditus*.

God remains hidden as the 'world come of age' constructs itself on the basis of a practical atheism and unbelief that God is concerned with suffering. Its counterfeit appeal to the suffering of the powerless lies in seeking to disguise the true nature of what is happening, most often because it is unaware itself of how the dynamics it has put in play influence life. The 'world come of age' promises to alleviate suffering through its technologies and political orders. It seeks to insulate us even from nature by the technologies of control. In the 'world come of age': 'The value of suffering as the forming of life through the threat of death is disregarded, even ridiculed.'[186]

Thus in the 'world come of age' we should not be surprised to see the emergence of totalitarianism because the claim to be able to keep us from suffering cloaks the desire to control.[187] In the soft totalitarianism of the 'world come of age', protection comes at the cost of our conscience. If we allow the authoritarian voices to do our thinking for us we will be safe: They present us with nothing other than dichotomies, either death or life, 'while they disguise their true nature with the mask of integrity.'[188] These are the choices we are given by those who seek to control us, either you are with us or you are against us, either you do things the way we want or you will die, as if the choices we are presented are the only ways that we can create the world. And all along religion is used to pacify persons to belief in idols who have

---

[185] Ibid., p. 97.

[186] Ibid., p. 129.

[187] This is a point that Stanley Hauerwas makes in his book *Performing the Faith: Bonhoeffer and the Practice of Nonviolence* (Grand Rapids, MI: Brazos Press, 2004), p. 54. Fn. 81.

[188] *Ethics*, p. 130.

been co-opted for purposes that serve to blind us to the true nature of the suffering we inflict on one another.

This is one reason why religionless Christianity is subversive to the arrangements of contemporary existence. It does not allow itself to be shaped by appeals to solidarity of race, religion or country; rather it challenges all orders of life that seek to maintain their status on something other than the sum of the law articulated by Jesus – love God and your neighbour as yourself. When the call to love the enemy is extinguished by the appeal to protect the homeland we have entered into pagan wisdom. The suffering of the Other in the world makes relative the culture in which I live. Loving the neighbour, even the enemy, is seen by Bonhoeffer as the beginning of a new creation, a social order that does not rest on the hierarchies which assign value in the world come of age. In this he never changes from the thoughts expressed in *Sanctorum Communio.*

Religionless Christianity is not a Christianity that seeks the totality and unity of all people into an enforced community. In this way, it becomes problematic for persons who desire the unity of all persons under one creed, whether that is a religious, political or economic creed. In the concerns of the atheistic state or the believing religion, it becomes acceptable to drop bombs and fly planes into skyscrapers because the suffering of the innocent does not really matter. We only seek to destroy those who will not be a part of our village in order that we may have peace. But it is definitely a peace that rests on the shaky foundations of coercion.

And so questions may be raised here about my assertions. At this point, the argument is that inasmuch as theology concerns itself primarily with concerns other than suffering it becomes detached from the reality of the world and subject to critique of being the manifestation of religion. But what of this appeal to suffering? Does it not have its own problems? Does this not offer a too romantic view of the noble sufferer? This call to endure suffering can become the oppression that religion itself has used to enslave others to its cultural masters. Who dares to tell me I must put myself into a place of vulnerability to the oppressor?

This valorization of suffering in the past has only served to make us more willing victims for the forces of dominance. Appeal to life in the 'sweet by and by' masks the destruction of those who take power in the 'bitter here and now'. Does not this embrace of suffering make us sheep for the taking at the hands of rapacious wolves? Most distinctly,

Bonhoeffer himself in the end responded to the suffering by participation in violence as the only way to stop the evil that choked his land. Why should our resistance not take the form of violence if Bonhoeffer himself was unable to live up to his own theology? We take up these concerns in the next chapter.

Chapter 6

CONFRONTING THE POWERS

We have been brought to a crucial moment in struggling with Dietrich Bonhoeffer. To put it bluntly, is religionless Christianity a viable option in a world that orders itself very well as if God did not exist? How does religionless Christianity respond in a situation where the political and economic elites create the conditions that cause so much suffering? If we live in the world as though God does not exist does this not take us into territory occupied by Nietzsche? If God is powerless in the world and only the suffering God can help, should we just raise our voices and hands in protest on behalf of the victims of the world's injustice and suffering? Should we not raise arms as well? If God on the cross defines the religionless Christian, how can he or she do anything other than stand mute in the face of suffering? Here is the intersection of reality, existence and faith that Bonhoeffer leads us to and this creates the great difficulty in appropriating his life for us.

We arrive at the question of the adequacy of Bonhoeffer for life in the world of terror and global conflict. Put simply, what use is the concern for the wounded if we are not ready to confront and stop those doing the wounding? This comes into focus in Bonhoeffer's life with his entry into the conspiracy. The commentaries on this are numerous, but at the core of those who rely on Bonhoeffer to justify war we find that it is for the protection of the innocent that they make the strongest appeal.

This alone stands as the only grounds on which to stand in agreeing with Bonhoeffer's participation in the coup to overthrow Hitler. Concern with the suffering of the oppressed and persecuted is the only position one can occupy and claim any legitimate connection to Bonhoeffer. Certainly one cannot stand on the justifications of empire or dominance in the world, even though those pretensions are cloaked with concern for the protection of the innocent. That the church has allowed herself to become compromised by the agendas of those who have no interest in pursuing alternatives to violence is evidence that the best motives become corrupted in the hands of those who have no interest in the demands of faith, or who interpret those demands differently than Bonhoeffer himself might have. How the church gets to the situation of legitimating what the state desires is a question of importance for our perspective.

BEFRIENDING THE EMPIRE

To begin, we must ask some questions regarding Christianity and its development. Though there are many nuances to this concern, I am most concerned with the dimensions that Christianity took that caused western civilization to be shaped the way it has. One way into this question is to ask how the cross of Christ, which was a symbol of political assassination, led to the development of a politically powerful Christian society that created a connection between governance and the people. How did the death of the criminal Jesus lead to the Christian religion becoming the force that would bind religion and empire into a unified body, the *corpus christianum?*

There are many interpretations of this. One interpretative trajectory starts with Jesus and sees a journey where the church struggles from a position of marginal existence and persecution by the empire. As these persecutions continued the church kept expanding into the world, taking more space by the power of its message. Because the empire exists for the good of its citizens, the expansion of Christianity could not be met solely by opposition, its impact had to be measured and thus incorporated into the life of the society. Once included within the empire, Christianity found itself needing to take responsibility for the empire's citizens once authority in the western regions of the empire disintegrated. This, of necessity, meant assuming responsibility for the state. Movement into this society encompassed necessary accommodations with the empire, even as it was on the verge of collapse. At some crucial step along the way Augustine entered the picture and with his brilliance constructed the narrative of the two cities to delineate the boundaries for this relationship.[189]

---

[189] For the fullest account of this see *The City of God*, Nicene and Post Nicene Fathers: First Series, Vol. II. Philip Schaff, ed. (Peabody, MA: Hendrickson Publishers, 1994).

As the historical development of this relationship played itself out, the inevitable tensions would become manifest as church and kingdom sought to develop their power in terms of the other.[190] These boundaries between society and its political orders, and the community of faith would always be contested, but Augustine did not believe that the church should subsume itself under the category of culture, rather he believed that the faithful have allegiances that transcend allegiances to state, and this creates the conditions for critique of the state when it behaves in a destructive way. The state has responsibilities to its citizens that must be monitored by the church in order that everyone might live as peacefully as possible.

The tensions inherent in this arrangement were found precisely in the use of violence to both protect the citizens of the state and coerce them when they did not conform to the dictates of the state. Christians had evidence that obedience to the state is found in scripture as, for example, in Paul's letter to the church at Rome, 13:1–7. Thus Christianity functioned as the glue that held society together in that unity known to us as the *corpus christianum*. Government was necessary in a fallen world so that chaos might not have the upper hand. This relationship held throughout the medieval era and into the sixteenth century.

Until the time of the Reformation the larger society of the Holy Roman Empire acted under the canopy of this tradition, invoked nowhere more exhaustively than in the doctrine of the divine right of kings where the rulers assumed the mantle of divine authority. Thus, for example, the church had no problem blessing the sword of the Emperor for fighting Muslim conquests during the centuries of conflict between these two faiths.

With the dawning of the Reformation this unity between political and ecclesiastical realms was broken, though the magisterial reformers sought in their own way to maintain the connection between the political and religious orders. Luther's doctrine of the two realms became employed by those who were trying to figure out a way that Christians should live in the new order. In Luther's conception, the state is divinely ordered, the instrument of divine providence where God prevails over the social order and is revealed as present in the civic affairs of humanity.

---

[190] Note, for instance, Bonhoeffer's account of this narrative in his section on 'Heritage and Decay' in *Ethics*, pp. 103–33.

Luther holds this pretty consistently in his writings, even though these can find nuanced changes throughout his life.[191] In the doctrine of the two realms Luther sought to address what he thought were the two most crucial aspects of human experience, justified and sinner, which centred all his thinking. Magistrates were beneficial to society in order to protect the orders of creation that God had established.

But if magistrates were instruments of God's providential care, if even tyrants were somehow the proper expression of God's sovereignty, then is anything other than obedience to these authorities called forth from Christians? Even more importantly for our purposes, if church and government exist in some type of interdependence on one another, each with its own domain of influence, then how does the church counter immoral and illegal actions of the state? It possesses no power to successfully resist the state, save the word of the gospel.

If the secular order commanded the Christian of the sixteenth century to participate in coercive violence to defeat the Turk, it did so for the protection of the neighbour. The logic of this position was so embedded in the cultural life that Bonhoeffer inhabited that the way was prepared for a Hitler. The religious dimensions of Christianity found in the state church tradition (and not just there, for the non-state supported church can be as miserably corrupted by the state as we have seen in the history of America) prepared the way for totalitarianism, since there were no internal possibilities for critique.

In fact, the point could be made that in Germany, especially, the way had been prepared for totalitarianism by the Lutheran heritage. This can be a complex story as well, but the Luther of the early 1520s disappeared with his movement to the prince's side of things in the Peasant's War of 1525. After this event, in which Luther encouraged slaughter of the oppressed for the sake of order, his conflicted legacy did not lead to resistance of tyrants, but admonitions for the political order to eradicate all threats to order, even when it came from the Anabaptists.

---

[191] Early on in the 1520s Luther was also overly optimistic concerning the secular realm's ability to be entrusted with the task of reforming corruption. Luther would become disillusioned to that possibility at the Diet of Worms. Succeeding documents such as, *On Temporal Authority: To What Extent It Should Be Obeyed*, were far more circumspect about the secular realm's ability to make God's presence a social reality. Still, even given his caution, he sided with the princes against the forces of chaos represented by the peasant's revolt.

I Pledge Allegiance to . . .?

That Bonhoeffer struggled precisely with this heritage is no surprise. It is found throughout all his writings from the earliest to the very last. How does a Christian live within her society and its institutions? At various times in his life, the answer to this question finds different expression. One of the places most examined by readers of Bonhoeffer was the address mentioned earlier, 'The Church and the Jewish Question.' He contends that the state exists by God's will for the purpose of law and order and the church exists solely from the Gospel. Bonhoeffer maintains the prerogatives of the state, but says the church has unconditional obligation to the victims of any ordering of society. What was so surprising about this address was that while Bonhoeffer gave the state its due place, he subverted this by arguing for active resistance by putting 'a spoke in the wheel' of the state.[192] This type of active resistance is serious business and can only occur when the state negates itself.

Bonhoeffer's struggles from the moment of this address in 1933 to the end of his life are reflective of showing how difficult it was to adequately respond to the Nazis. If your theological tradition has been constructed in such a way that the benefit of the doubt has already been placed on the side of the state's legitimacy and existence, no real compelling argument can be made against the behaviour of the state, unless its actions become so overwhelmingly egregious they can no longer be ignored. If Christians accord the state the status of an order of creation, response to business as usual becomes difficult.

This raises questions as to the form the state assumes in present day terms. The social and political arrangements made in that part of the 'world come of age' known to us in the West, proceed from the pragmatic basis that religious belief should be fenced off from public expression. The exception to this might be a civil religion that serves the cause of the state to glue people to one another in a type of national unity. Given this, perhaps it might be wiser for religionless Christianity to proceed in the realization that the state has no interest in faithfulness to Christ and that the faithful can entertain another option, a non-religious option regarding the state.

If civil religion functions, even in the state hostile to it, to construct a sacred canopy over our transient political orders, then perhaps a

---

[192] *NRS*, p. 225.

religionless Christianity could think about its responsibility vis-à-vis the state differently than tradition and custom has shaped us to think. Perhaps if we are attentive to the ways in which the political order has compromised Christianity historically we might discover something in the political order itself that should be regarded from the space of enormous suspicion.

If the reality under which the community of faith lives is the Incarnate One and the world lives out its existence in direct contradiction to the revelation of God embodied in Christ perhaps we ought to question if, in this historical moment, the church's ministry to the world is not that of critique and prophetic witness. Faithfulness to the cross at this point may call forth an analysis of the economic and political structures that reveal their impact on the suffering of the world.

In the 'world come of age' the state becomes a community that is self-interpreting. Locked in the logics we mentioned earlier, it resists those voices that call it to accountability to perspectives other than the one it decides for itself. Rooted in nothing other than the logics of the market or power, the state has an ambiguous moral grounding. There are those good souls who labour valiantly to construct a space of moral authority and influence for the state, but oftentimes this becomes suspect when the state enters into conflict with other nations that pursue the same goals of resource management or social order.

Because the state operates on logics that are distinctly not Christian in any but the most religious sense (i.e., justification for its behaviour) it becomes enveloped in its own justifications, which in a nominally Christian nation assume the patina of religious justification.[193] Thus in times of conflict, tension or decision making, there are few alternatives for the state to consider other than the ones which its prior rationalities have given it. Certain choices become necessities. 'We had no other choice,' we are told, when in fact there were many choices, but only a select few which the state wished to pursue.

One problem with the contemporary democratic state is that the elites who really control the levers of power claim to be acting on behalf of the will of the people. What was previously legitimated through appeal to the sovereignty of God, acting through the king, has become in the 'world come of age' reduced to the authority of the

---

[193] This is not to suggest that the United States is in any sense a 'Christian' nation, but the history and tradition of the country have lent themselves to a narrative that finds appeal to many in the Christian churches.

sovereignty of the people. But this is where democracy itself, as presently constituted, raises questions even as those who use it to accomplish their aims seek to absolutize it. What type of democracy takes shape among us if it is but a collection of citizens who are reduced to the status of individuals acting in self-interests and regulated through military force or the unquestioned assumptions operative in supposedly liberal democracies?[194] Is this political community one that should be uncritically accepted, or one that should be called into question?

What concrete form of question would the community of Jesus Christ ask about the 'world come of age' if it had followed a different narrative trajectory from the one we are now considering? Though this is a speculative question in some measure because we have what history has given us, it is one that Bonhoeffer himself was asking as he sat in prison. Bonhoeffer believed that the church must find a new way of being in the world, a non-religious way that walks a different path from the one that baptizes the political orders with the waters of divine authority. He suggested that the church does not have to accept the temptation offered it by the state to bless its agenda with divine approval.

In the part of the writings in *Ethics* under the heading of 'Heritage and Decay' Bonhoeffer contends that the church is returning to its historical genesis as the West is becoming hostile to Christ. He writes as one who has lived in the age of Christian hegemony in culture, participated in the benefits, but now sees that the rug is being pulled out from under the old order:

> The corpus christianum has broken apart. The corpus Christi stands over against a hostile world. The church must bear witness to Jesus Christ as living lord, and it must do so in a world that has turned away from Christ after knowing him.[195]

He continues that in the midst of the ruins of western civilization: 'The more the church holds to its central message, the more effective it is. Its suffering is infinitely more dangerous to the spirit of destruction than the political power that it may still retain.' The church serves the need of the world most when: 'It forces the custodians of power in particular to listen and change their ways.'[196] Where, today, do we see this confrontation of the custodians of power?

---

[194] Long, p. 249.
[195] *Ethics*, p. 132.
[196] Ibid., pp. 132–33.

How Does Christ Take Form in the World Today?

This is not an entirely new space that Bonhoeffer occupies, though it shifted throughout his life. We recall once more that how Christ takes form in the world, how we are shaped by Christ, is a touchstone for Bonhoeffer's life. He is a theologian because he believes that theology is a crucial aspect of this shaping. Through its visions the community forms itself in readiness for the life of God to be made visible on the earth. These communities formed by Christ assume distinct shape in the world. In *Sanctorum Communio,* Bonhoeffer says we become the people we are because Christ creates and holds this community of persons together through the Holy Spirit creating a new creation: 'Rather, God established the reality of the church, of humanity pardoned in Jesus Christ – not religion, but revelation, *not religious community, but church.* This is what the reality of Jesus Christ means.'[197]

This is the goal that Bonhoeffer pursues, the desire that Christ might assume concrete form on earth. And even though he lived in the midst of a dark and challenging time, he does not lose sight of this as the most important thing. He struggles with the place of the Sermon on the Mount, faithful obedience, discipleship and Christian responsibility for the world. In his Christology lectures delivered in the early 1930s the reality of Christ becomes the centre of history through the church. At this period of his life, he employed some measure of the two spheres thinking to argue for the perspective that the church is a servant to the state without which the state would destroy itself.[198]

But as matters developed in Germany the church's choices became so stark that Christ's concrete form on earth through the church becomes somewhat muddled. Where does one find Christ in the midst of the glorification of the Nazis, of swastikas flying at the altars of Christianity? This was no theoretical question because the struggle between the German Christians and the Confessing Church was precisely this question. Is there a true and false manifestation of Christ-existing-as-community? The decisions taken by the church would have life and death consequences. Unfortunately we have ample witness to the failure of the church to be the bearer of Christ to the world at this point.

---

[197] Dietrich Bonhoeffer, *Sanctorum Communio: A Theological Study of the Sociology of the Church*, ed. Clifford J. Green, trans. Reinhard Krauss and Nancy Lukens, (Minneapolis, MN: Fortress Press) p. 153.

[198] This is also the perspective in *NRS.*

As Bonhoeffer struggled with this, he responded in a number of different ways, sometimes by choosing exile from Germany in London or America, but ultimately he positioned himself to share in the sufferings of his people. During this struggle, Bonhoeffer shaded his theology in different directions as can be seen through the writings of *Discipleship* and *Ethics* and *Letters and Papers from Prison.* In the earlier moments, he is pretty clear and decisive about how faith functions in response to Christ's call; 'From the human point of view there are countless possibilities of understanding and interpreting the Sermon on the Mount. Jesus knows only one possibility: simply go and obey. Do not interpret or apply, but do it and obey. That is the only way Jesus' word is really heard.'[199]

He continues in this clarity to say that we not attain to this ideal in our own power, but we begin by acting and trusting God who will honour our movement into the world: 'The word of Jesus keeps its honor, its strength, and power among us only by our acting on it. Then a storm can sweep over the house, but it cannot tear apart the unity with Jesus created by his word.'[200]

But the storm did sweep over the house and even as Bonhoeffer was writing these words he knew of the possibility of what could happen to his society. Yet, even so, he warns that to negate the word of God, to say no to the Sermon on the Mount, means we will find ourselves swept away by the storm: 'Hence, when the storm comes, I will lose the word quickly and I will learn that in truth I never really had faith.'[201] It is still one of the most debated questions in the story of Bonhoeffer as to whether the storm did cause him to lose touch with this aspect of his faith with his entrance into the conspiracy.

As mentioned previously, Bonhoeffer's understanding of how the church takes form during the time he is writing from Finkenwalde connects the church and state only tangentially. The community of faith resides as ' . . . a colony of strangers far away from home, a community of foreigners enjoying the hospitality of the host country in which they live, obeying the laws and honoring the authorities.'[202] How does this band of pilgrims, locked into their own piety, offer much in the way of help to the wounded? Later Bonhoeffer would indicate that

---

[199] *Discipleship*, p. 181.
[200] Ibid., p. 182.
[201] Ibid.
[202] Ibid., p. 250.

he saw the problems of this book, though he still stood by what he had written.[203]

Life under the regime would create great difficulties in Bonhoeffer's life. The closing of Finkenwalde, the conscription of most of the students into the military, the total collapse of the Confessing Church; all these things signalled an effective end to any type of ecclesial resistance. The theologian of community found himself without a strong community of support within the visible church. Bonhoeffer himself suffered internal exile by order of the Gestapo and was only able to maintain contact with members of Finkenwalde through letters circulated among former students.

As events would unfold after his return from America, Bonhoeffer would find himself in a different type of community. This community was also a community of resistance, though their agenda was decidedly different from the community of faith. Through family connections such as Hans von Dohnanyi, Bonhoeffer entered into the conspiracy to overthrow Hitler, by force if necessary, and wrestled with how to understand his participation in that community.

Most certainly this community's concerns were not the ones that Bonhoeffer had been addressing. While there may have been some concern for the suffering that the world was enduring there was as much, if not more, concern over what was going to happen to Germany if matters were allowed to continue. The various factions that made up the resistance were desperately seeking ways to salvage the Germany they knew even as they realized that Hitler had overextended himself with the push into the Soviet Union.[204] Obedience to God in Christ did not really form the basis on which persons in this community acted, though Bonhoeffer would believe that God was there.

Bonhoeffer himself was rethinking the entire two spheres tradition as he had inherited it. He knew that this was a sword that cut both ways. It not only failed to fortify an effective resistance to the pretensions of the state, but the church itself had collapsed under its weight and had become invisible. Allegiance to the state had trumped faithfulness to Christ because the habits of almost 2,000 years of tradition had become so ingrained few saw other possibilities.

---

[203] *LPP*, p. 369.

[204] Larry Rasmussen has an interesting account of this in his book *Reality and Resistance*, pp. 174–211. For a theological rendering of this see Clifford Green's *Bonhoeffer: A Theology of Sociality*, rev. ed. (Grand Rapids, MI: Eerdmans, 1999), pp. 304–27.

What remained, the visible church, was in truth a manifestation of the religion of Christianity. Its marks were all too apparent – a theology that justified the ruling order, a triumphalism that glorified its nation's militarism, an ethnocentricity that held the nation as uniquely connected to the divine, and a religious particularity that interpreted the superiority of its own religion as the justification for the destruction of the religious Other which existed in its midst. A racist and nihilistic ideology prepared for by a religion blind to its own reality continues to scar the memory of humankind.

Christianity had much to answer for and Bonhoeffer, to his credit, recognized that he shared this heritage. However, unlike most of us confronted by our complicity in evil, he understood that his nation and, by extension, he himself were responsible. This constitutes the ground under which Bonhoeffer moved into the conspiracy. No matter how much we may try and romanticize this in our day, the reality is that Bonhoeffer's participation in the attempt to overthrow Hitler represented nothing other than the abject failure of the church in those circumstances to offer any alternative to the evil in its midst.

As we read his writings during this time we cannot help but be profoundly moved by the internal pain Bonhoeffer must have been experiencing. His identification with the sufferings of God permeates the texts he is working on. How God calls the disciple in the midst of this moral confusion is not mere intellectual abstraction. Bonhoeffer is still dealing with '*how Christ may take form among us today and here.*'[205] The difficulty for Bonhoeffer is that all the ideas he had about nonviolence did not help in ridding the world of Hitler. And as he tries to deal with his responsibility for this, he is at the same time grieving the loss of any community that could have kept this from happening in the first place. Without a community that could have kept Hitler from gaining power, without a larger society that could have made Christ truly visible, Bonhoeffer had no support to do what he knew the Gospel calls of the disciple of Christ.

Isolated by the state and the church and trying to assume responsibility for his role in the Nazi regime under extreme pressure, Bonhoeffer moved to the only other community open to him, the conspiracy. In the end he took a path that did negate his earlier beliefs, but it was not necessarily because the faith expressed was wrong, it was more that no community existed which had been formed by the disciplines and

---

[205] *Ethics*, 99.

practices necessary to sustain it in the midst of such political force. More than Bonhoeffer's failure, it was the history of Christianity itself that had aligned itself with the ruling orders unquestionably that led to this. Bonhoeffer himself took responsibility for this choice and never counted it as a brave and heroic step, but a necessary one, given the circumstances.

Thus Have We Made the World

It is curious, then, that, as we saw in the first chapter, Bonhoeffer becomes employed by those in the present time to justify war, or specifically, becomes used by Christians in America to justify their particular response to the 'war on terror'. He should stand as a sign of the church's failures to bear witness to the Gospel of Jesus Christ when a radical witness was most needed. Yet this failure was in some measure contained within Christianity itself as a religious community, especially the way that Judaism became defined through interpretation of Christian scriptures. Bonhoeffer's participation in the plot to assassinate Hitler should be the last thing we think of when we wonder how we are to respond to the current time of conflict. This failure of Christianity to side with the victims of injustice should never be allowed to stand as the normative response to tyranny.

For those who are inclined to make Bonhoeffer's actions normative then they should be prepared to follow Bonhoeffer to the Golgatha he walked. His movement into the conspiracy was accompanied by his willing acceptance of the guilt of his nation for the destruction it had wrought on the world. He accepted responsibility for what the nation had done and his action in the conspiracy reflected his accepting the guilt of the sinful actions of the state. This was not a move that absolved Bonhoeffer from the sinfulness of the action (though Bonhoeffer does write that the true disciple moves beyond good and evil), rather it was an act of guilt-filled contrition for the crimes that were allowed to become manifest in a supposedly Christian nation.

This necessitates painful and difficult questions for those who use Bonhoeffer as an example for action in the beginning of what promises to be a long and generational struggle in contemporary times, 'the war on terror'. It is called a war because those who have the most interest in keeping it going need the rhetoric of war to marshal persons to give their lives. But on all sides the underlying issues are not dealt with at all, thus ensuring that attack with be met with attack, and blood revenge, if we cannot bring ourselves to act in different ways, will become the driving force for the foreseeable future.

In the midst of this many Christians do not see the need for confession of sins. They accept the notion of the nation's innocence. Like those of Bonhoeffer's time we make it a point to not resist the forces that presently drive this conflict. We have no complicity in these orders, we tell ourselves, and thus we take no responsibility for what our nation does. Are we even able to recognize our role in the actions taken by the nation to secure its own dominance?

I exist within the current, but quickly fading, empire of America (there will be others after us) and as far as I can tell there is little to no Christian witness that would indicate we are prepared to enter into the absence of God that Bonhoeffer experienced later in his life. To take this step would necessitate looking without self-deception at the behaviour of deceitfulness and lies that has corrupted political life in America. It would mean telling the truth about what colonial behaviour looks like to a culture that not only refuses to hear it, but works overtime at denying that there is a truth in anything other than the narrative that America never has its own interests at heart when it acts. We only desire to help others achieve the blessings of liberty. Citizens of other nations also have their own political and social orders to address, so in this way American Christianity is not unique.

One truth that does not get told is that the 'war on terror' functions as a means of control. It is certainly the case that the West does have enemies, that there are those who want our destruction, and that we must deal with these threats to the world community. As we face these concerns, though, is it the case that we have responded wisely to the destruction of our time? Is violence the only response to our situation? There are truths that are not being told because they are not believed.

That the political order may have other agendas than protecting the innocent is one truth. Another is the truth about war. Because war gives our life meaning, human beings will still continue to resort to it almost as a first choice rather than a final one, no matter what our public rhetoric says. It is curious that humans will often follow and support any political order which, despite its public protestations, often uses war as a way to exert its dominance and political will.

But Bonhoeffer himself well understood the destructive powers unleashed by war. He knew the cost incurred by society when the first recourse to conflict is the hard power of war. He also knew the moral bankruptcy in calling everything justified as long as it serves the cause of your people. War assumes the shape it currently does essentially because the 'world come of age' relies on its own logics and rationalities, not because it follows the cause of Christ.[206] There may exist within the destructive energies of war provisional goods, such as a strategic advantage for a nation, or access to resources, or even overthrow of the tyrant, but these are not by necessity the goods of the community of all beings which God has created. Oftentimes the cost in loss of life outweighs any benefit war may have brought. Too often the right hope of human beings – to enact justice, to stop oppression, to protect the vulnerable – is turned towards the wrong desire. Once placed there, the habits of destruction tend to replicate themselves.[207]

War itself is a destructive force that destroys persons, communities and nations. It sets in motion future events that will keep the momentum going towards more violence. Bonhoeffer was only too aware of this and numerous places in his writings we find his judgements of war do not offer anything like unqualified acceptance. Reading the entirety of Bonhoeffer's work leads more to the realization that Bonhoeffer saw very clearly the danger of war to the life of the world, especially in its modern form.

In an address to the Youth Peace Conference in what was then Czechoslovakia on 26 July 1932 he deals with the issue of the struggle for peace and weaves together a discussion on the concerns of truth, justice and peace. He is careful to say that these terms are never static, but that there may be times when they are contested, resulting in the

---

[206] *Ethics*, pp. 109–10. In the section *Heritage and Decay* Bonhoeffer has some profound insights about the way that war has mutated over the centuries in the West and rightly understands that war can become total, not limited, in its defence of national self-preservation. Everything is right because it serves the needs of one's own people. It was Christian faith that renounced the effective but criminal means – killing of innocents, torture, extortion – of war, but when faith in God is lost people feel compelled to make these means legitimate and thus 'war of total annihilation in which everything that serves one's own cause, even crime, is justified, and in which the enemy, armed or unarmed, is regarded as a criminal.'

[207] There are some horrific letters to Bonhoeffer from former students from the Russian front that speak of the horrors and destruction of the soul of soldiers in the midst of war. There are heartbreaking stories of soldiers who engaged in slaughter because they believed it was the most expedient thing to do in the circumstances. The letter from Erwin Sander to Bonhoeffer written from the Russian front on 4 February 1942 is an example of what has happened to this former student of Finkenwalde. The juxtaposition of killing and comforts of Christ are startling and disturbing. Dietrich Bonhoeffer, *Conspiracy and Imprisonment: 1940–1945*, Dietrich Bonhoeffer Works, vol. 16, Mark S. Brocker, ed., Lisa Dahill, trans. (Minneapolis, MN: Fortress Press, 2006), pp. 251–52.

need to struggle for them. This struggle can in some ways serve as openness to the revelation in Christ because it serves to break apart a rigid order, even the totalitarian order of peace. He goes on to warn, however, that this struggle does not in itself justify war:

> There is, however, a very widespread, extremely dangerous error about today that the *justification of struggle* already contains the justification of war, affirms war in principle. The right of war can be derived from the right of struggle as little as the use of torture may be derived from the necessity of legal procedures in human society.[208]

He says that war destroys body and soul and results in terrible and total annihilation that must be resisted and rejected by the church. This is not the only space where Bonhoeffer condemns war in robust terms. He is insightful enough to realize that there is a totalitarian peace which brings peace at the cost of capitulation to a particular way of understanding that is historically conditional. The order of peace that purports to usher in truth and justice can rest on a foundation of lies and injustice. Those who claim that truth and justice are present where there is peace secured by coercive means must be met with skepticism. As Miroslav Volf explains, there are different orders of this peace and one rests on shaky foundations: 'In Pilate's world, truth and justice were *fruits* of Caesar's sword. In Jesus' kingdom, truth and justice were *alternatives* to Caesar's sword.'[209]

For those who are quick to prescribe war as the only avenue to protect the innocent no other option seems possible. Partially this is because we do not adequately understand the extent to which our social orders have become dominated by militarism. Because we do not choose to see the shape that society has taken and the acids generated by the 'world come of age' eating away at the good creation of God, we lose the ability to discern any other avenue available to us to confront the forces that shape the world.

This goes to the secular telos mentioned earlier because once we are absorbed into our own rationalities we continue to operate out of the logics they give us. Bonhoeffer himself was caught in these logics even though theologically he very strongly argued for a way of escape for the church in much of his writing. But once the ends of stopping

---

[208] *NRS*, p. 170. This address, read in its entirety is really remarkable considering the youth of Bonhoeffer at the time.

[209] Miroslav Volf, *Exclusion and Embrace*, p. 275.

tyranny become prescribed in such a way that war or violence are seen as inevitable, the momentum becomes inexorably set. It is the rationality of hell.

When the argument is made that self-defense, or the defense of the innocent, is embedded within the moral order in such a way that necessitates violence, no other way becomes possible to respond to the situation. Even more, the Incarnation is negated to the position that only Jesus' humanity is capable of living out of the goodness of God and we are of such a nature that we are unable to fulfil God's desire for how we are to live in the world.

No more are we enabled to hear the perspective of Bonhoeffer who contends that God became human so that we may become more fully human in response to grace and thus conformed to Christ, the form of all reality.[210] Is the church faithful to Christ only when it is expedient? Do we really want to follow Bonhoeffer into the abyss of despair he suffered when he took the step of seeking to overthrow the government? When the church fails to mitigate the violence unleashed from within its national borders is tyrannicide of one's own democratically elected leader (Hitler did win the popular vote) the only option open to us? Put in such bald terms the question is obscene. One stands on shaky ground to argue that this singular moment of struggle on Bonhoeffer's part should ever be made into a normative path of action for Christians.

Perhaps this brings us to a searching discrimination about the way our responsibility to the world works as Christians. In the same address referenced above Bonhoeffer had some thoughts about how the church responds to the world: 'What the sacrament is for the preaching of the Gospel, the knowledge of firm reality is for the preaching of the sacrament. *Reality is the sacrament of command.*'[211] That reality is the God revealed in Jesus Christ. If reality is to be interpreted through these lenses then perhaps another way than violence exists whereby the church fights for the wounded. In part this takes place by its willingness to suffer the wounds of the wounded themselves. This, however, is not a move to passivity and surrender to the powers, rather it constitutes a place of profound power in powerlessness.

---

[210] This is one of the crucial centers of Bonhoeffer's theology and recurs often. A powerful example of his struggle how to place God within the world is covered in the section 'Christ, Reality, and the Good', in *Ethics*.

[211] *NRS*, p. 164.

The church can respond in its ability and willingness to tell the world something true about itself. The church can question the reality of the world and the means by which it organizes itself. The world itself is scarcely able to understand the ways in which destruction has become embedded within its primary assumptions. The church, which should live free of these assumptions, inasmuch as they do not rest on the creation of the community of forgiveness of sins and reconciliation of the enemy, can offer a different vision for how society constructs itself. Yet the path that has brought us here historically makes this extremely difficult, not the least because we have not cultivated the necessary disciplines and practices to offer much resistance as a community to the prevailing orders.

When the political ideologies that constitute nation–states today seek to create systems of control through self-replicating, self-justifying political and economic systems they establish boundaries that only allow the church one voice – participate the way we demand or be relegated to obscurity or derision. Embrace the reality we conceive and work to make self-evident, or be consigned to the ranks of those who are irrelevant.

Does the church aid and protect the suffering best by worshipping at the altars of the powers of the state? The church does not exist for itself or even the cultures within which it lives. It exists for God and the possibility that in this world there is a manifestation of God's desire for the creation. In its most profound moments the church stands immersed in this life as a witness to the ultimate in the midst of the penultimate. This is whole thrust of Bonhoeffer's section on 'Christ, Reality, and Good' found in *Ethics*. This calls from the Christian a different way of dealing with the real world, because the narrative of the Gospel creates conditions on the ground of the world itself that the 'world come of age' does not acknowledge.

If the vision that the community of faith offers calls the 'world come of age' into question then this must happen in concrete ways. Bonhoeffer himself would have been very careful about making these distinct ways concretized, set in stone, unable to respond to the call of God in particular times, but he was never afraid to address the world in its precise form:

> It is as though all the powers of the world had conspired together against peace; money, business, the lust for power, indeed even the love for the Fatherland have been pressed into the service of hate. Hate of nations, hate of men against their own countrymen . . . Events are coming to a head more terribly than ever before – *millions hungry*, men with cruelly deferred and unfulfilled

wishes, desperate men who have nothing to lose but their lives and will lose nothing in losing them – humiliated and degraded nations who cannot get over their shame – *political extreme against political extreme, fanatic against fanatic,* idol against idol, and behind it all a world which bristles with weapons as never before, a world which feverishly arms to guarantee peace through arming, a world whose idol has become the word 'security' – a world without sacrifice, full of mistrust and suspicion, because past fears are still with it . . .[212]

Bonhoeffer goes on to write that the demonic power of his age was so strong that polite discussions, or new organizations were not going to be enough to drive out the darkness.

Concretely, Bonhoeffer believed that one of the major tasks of the church is to confront the 'world come of age' in its own godlessness. Resistance may mean that we raise questions about how decisions have been taken and paths have been followed in the past that have led us to this historical moment. These questions should be asked to uncover and reveal the truth of what we are dealing with presently.

For example, we might ask what are the true concerns behind the will to power we presently see playing themselves out in the 'war on terror'? Could it be the case that those who have power wish to impose their worldview on the Middle East so that they may gain control of energy resources? Or, as may also be the case, that there are those who wish to impose an ideological perspective on the Middle East in order that certain political and economic orders might remain dominant? How has the nation that I live within sought to extend its power in the world and where has that caused the deaths of the innocents? What historical paths have we followed in our dealing with others that have been done in the name of altruism, but actually it was corporate interests that were at stake?

Specifically, in Iraq, were we not complicit in arming and supporting the dictator we would later dispose in the name of freedom? Did we not arm and supply Osama Bin Laden in Afghanistan thus creating the violence we confront? The answer may come that radical Islam would be on our doorstep anyway given its pretensions to power, but we prepared the way. Did this not unleash a new level of violence and hatred that will take generations to extinguish? Is not the future being prepared for us now by our flawed military approaches to resolving conflict? Where does responsibility rest for the terrors that undoubtedly lie in our future? And, more importantly, how does religionless Christianity respond?

---

[212] *NRS*, pp. 186–87.

We live within systems of being that operate on the extensions of power through means of bureaucracies and technological prowess. It is these systems that have laid down the tracks upon which we find ourselves racing towards the future. They have certainly shaped the world we know now and unless they are confronted they will lead us into more war, conflict and destruction. Does religionless Christianity have anything of value to contribute to this?

As mentioned before, these systems are grounded in a logic that excludes the possibility that God has desires for the way in which we are to live. By the renunciation of any divine intention for creation, any expressions of political or social life we construct results in our continuing captivity to and self-destruction by these forces. By arguing and accepting the case for pragmatism, 'This is the way the world is, get realistic' we acquiesce to a self-defeating proposition.[213] The wisdom of the 'world come of age' argues this is the way the world is and we must deal with it as it is, not as a naïve idealism wishes it to be. Idealism has sometimes led to as much violence as realism ever has. And, there is a germ of truth in this concept, but it is a truth that does not consider another possibility.[214] We are the ones who created the world the way it is, and we are the ones who can change it.

[213] Along these lines, there is a telling letter from Paul Lehmann to Bonhoeffer in 2 August 1941 in which Lehmann says that his pacifism was too naïve and romantic. He now recognized the role of government to maintain order in the face of chaos, especially in light of the international situation. But absent from Lehmann's understanding is the possibility that the order the democratic political orders demand may themselves be problematic. *Conspiracy and Imprisonment*, pp. 196–201.

[214] Bonhoeffer explores this other alternative in the address at Fanø, 'The Church and the Peoples of the World.' I am tempted to copy the entire address, however Bonhoeffer writes:

> Peace on earth is not a problem, but a commandment given at Christ's coming. There are two ways of reacting to this command from God: the unconditional, blind obedience of action, or the hypocritical question of the Serpent: 'Yea, hath God said . . .?' This question is the mortal enemy of obedience, and therefore the mortal enemy of all real peace. 'Has God not said? Has God not understood human nature well enough to know that wars must occur in this world, like laws of nature? Must God not have meant that we should talk about peace, to be sure, but that is not to be literally translated into action? Must God not really have said that we should work for peace, of course, but also make ready tanks and poison gas for security?' And then perhaps the most serious question: 'Did God say you should not protect your own people?' Did God say you should leave your own a prey to the enemy?' No, God did not say all that. (*NRS*, p. 289)

There is a scene in the movie, 'The Mission' starring Robert DeNiro and Jeremy Irons that occurs at the end of the movie. The emissary of the Roman Catholic Church has just received the news reports of the devastation and destruction of the Guarani Indians of South America. He had been sent to South America to mediate a dispute between Spain and Portugal that threatened the church in Europe. As events unfolded the displacement and slaughter of thousands of natives takes place. One character, played by DeNiro, is an ex-mercenary who becomes a brother in the order through the efforts of a priest played by Jeremy Irons. In the ensuing struggle, he fights for the Guarani Indian with the way he knows best, violence. The priest fights for the Indian the way he knows best, through suffering love.

In the end neither survives the destruction that ensues, but both live out of their desire to protect the innocent. As the cardinal hears of his priests being murdered and the natives being destroyed he asks the political emissaries if this slaughter was necessary. One of them responds, that, yes, it was given the emissary's decrees:

> 'You had no other alternative, your Eminence. We must work in the world. The world is thus.' At this the papal emissary responds, 'No, Señor Hontar, thus have we made the world. Thus have I made it.'

In this world making of ours religionless Christianity can hold a mirror to the 'world come of age' and ask why it has become so captive to rationalities of death that it is unable to pursue other courses of action than the violence to which it has become addicted. Religionless Christianity can free itself enough from the cultural forms around it to immerse itself into those forms in a new and entirely different way. The religionless Christian can untether from the assumptions that drive the violence that continues to tear the 'world come of age' asunder, but this requires its own type of conversion.

Bonhoeffer saw that Christianity had become incomprehensible to the citizens of modernity, save in its religious guise. The territory mapped and travelled by modernity cannot recognize the revelation of God in Christ. We certainly do not anticipate a Christianity that continually subverts the ruling ethos of a culture captured in its own prison. This is not the Christianity that persons use to legitimate responses to the world that assume violence as the only means of bringing about peace. A religionless Christianity could well take the form of public resistance to the 'way things are'.

This public response can be offensive to a number of parties. It is disturbing to those who seek to remove all religious claims from the public arena because they rightly see the damage done to the powers that dominate society if the claims of Christians were actually to be taken seriously. The Christian call to love your enemy is the call to a creation of a new order that does not take its justification from the ruling ethos of society as constituting the acceptable parameters of existence. It is offensive sometimes to those whose authentic concern is for the wounded because they cannot find in its non-violent form a way to stop the oppressor. It is also offensive to those who believe that their nation is an idol to be obeyed and not another fallen and flawed structure of sinful human beings.

Thus we come back to the crux of how we respond to those forces that cause the wounds. Love doesn't really seem to be an option for many because it is so ineffectual to the pragmatic mind. Better to just put a bullet into the oppressor so that they don't have the ability to wound again. Yet, here again, the question is not being asked about what responsibility we share for the appearance of the political and economic forces that act in our name. How has our participation, or our acquiescence led to the world we confront today? What lies have we accepted in order to be left in peace?

Looking historically at Germany it becomes easy in hindsight to see how this unfolded. With distance we can say we would never allow such a thing to happen to us. Our society would never allow torture or murder or disappearances of people, or at least this is what we tell ourselves. Because we fail to see this in ourselves, that we also do the same thing, we repeat our self-destructive actions. One wonders what horror it will take for us to realize that in the 'world come of age' self-justification on the basis of 'saving' the world ultimately dooms those who stand in the way of 'the greater good'. The greater the utopian idea that the elites devise, the greater the list of causalities they leave in their wake.

As we have previously seen, from his prison cell Bonhoeffer wrote that confronting the powers may not come from our power, but from the powerlessness of God. In fact, he saw this as the only way out. For him Jesus Christ stands as an authentic embodiment of God precisely because he was willing to accept the unexpected and unanticipated way of powerlessness and suffering. Jesus stood at the intersection of reality and interpretation to offer new possibility to the world:

> All that we may rightly expect from God, and ask him for, is to be found in Jesus Christ. The God of Jesus Christ has nothing to do with what God as we imagine him could do and ought to do. If we are to learn what God promises and what he

fulfills, we must persevere in quiet meditations on the life, sayings, deeds, sufferings, and death of Jesus.[215]

In the contemporary world, we might ask if such ideas legitimize violence. Does not this embrace of powerlessness mean we acquiesce to the oppressor? Nietzsche raises precisely this point in *The Antichrist* when he says the ethic of Jesus emerges from his pathological resistance to all contact with reality. Placing all hope on an inner world, a negation of reality, Jesus makes a virtue of necessity. Someone who is essentially without power cannot really exercise power, so they call on the powerful to give up their power. It is decadence to preach the poor, meek, blind and peacemakers are more blessed than the rich, strong and powerful.

Given this, how can these prison writings of Bonhoeffer offer us anything of value in our contemporary struggles? How could it not be the case that Bonhoeffer says we must stand by God in God's hour of suffering because he himself is suffering? Bonhoeffer doesn't say a true word about God because it is his suffering he is actually talking about. Powerlessness, weakness, suffering and death are mere aspects of his captivity. Are these the projections of his current situation, placed on God? What could be any clearer than the realization that the so-called power of weakness is uncovered as yet another delusion and refusal to face reality? Disillusioned by the failure to kill the tyrant and the collapse of his faith community, beset by guilt over his involvement in the conspiracy, Bonhoeffer is writing about himself, not God.

These are powerful critiques, and most often offered from within the rationalities of the 'world come of age'. But Bonhoeffer believed that immersion in the world was a necessary condition for faithfulness and an avenue for the entrance of something different and subversive in the world. The weakness and suffering which authentic faith endures does not create more willing victims of oppression. As we saw previously, faith has the potential to create communities that show the structures of power their own godless actions:

> But what does this life look like, this participation in the powerlessness of God in the world? I will write about that next time, I hope. Just one more point for today. When we speak of God in a 'non-religious' way, we must speak of him in such a way that the godlessness of the world is not in some way concealed, but rather revealed, and thus exposed to an unexpected light. The world that has come of

[215] *LPP*, p. 391.

age is more godless, and perhaps for that very reason nearer to God, than the world before its coming of age.[216]

As Christ exists for others and we participate in Christ, we experience divine presence when we exist for others as well. Though we may share the sufferings of others in the world, this does not mean we are at the mercy of the world. The community of the cross offers a new and different way of being in the world, the way of forgiveness of sins and reconciliation with God. Because forgiveness and reconciliation have been so rooted in an individual piety the radical nature of these ideas in society remain hidden. Sometimes they emerge with such things as the Truth and Reconciliation Commission in South Africa, but the world by and large does not value this form of response to evil, suffering and violence.

If nothing else the power of forgiveness and reconciliation as concrete realities has the potential to create a community that lives such an alternative to violence that refusal to participate in life according to the world's perspectives becomes subversive. This is why there can be so much hatred expressed to those who fail to participate in the justification of a nation's actions. The church has the potential to live in such a way that its very presence and being in the world calls all ideological and self-aggrandizing power into question.

The communities of Christ can be defined by worldly solidarity and by their cultivation of what Bonhoeffer called 'arcane disciplines'. The cultivation of these disciplines forms the necessary structure to the community of faith and provides the sustenance for the type of costly discipleship necessary in troubled times. We will have more to say about the contours of this community in the next chapter, but for now I want to make the suggestion that in the way of this powerlessness, found in religionless Christianity, we may find a power that has always existed which can confront those forces that seek the destruction of God's good creation. This power asks different questions and pursues a costly grace, a grace that puts one on the side of those who are voiceless in the world.

[216] *LPP*, p. 362.

Chapter 7

WHAT IS CHRISTIANITY FOR US TODAY?

In May of 1944 Dietrich Bonhoeffer offered some perspectives upon the occasion of the baptism of Eberhard Bethge's son. 'Thoughts on the Day of the Baptism of Dietrich Wilhelm Rüdiger Bethge' is a profoundly poignant document coming from Bonhoeffer's captivity in Tegel. It contains some interesting reflections and insights into Bonhoeffer's mind at the time. He assesses the world that had been constructed in the name of reason, and tells his godson that this world is controlled by forces against which reason can do nothing. This world lives in the tensions between the massive organization of bureaucracies mentioned earlier, and the personal lives of those who are subjected to the collective's will. The direction that the world takes between the impersonality of bureaucracies that do not much care for the lives of the individuals that comprise it, and the personality of those very lives, moves on its own inexorable way without regard for anything other than the organization.

But Bonhoeffer was sure of one thing – the direction matters took would be shaped by whether the powerful and elites who run these vast institutions were prepared to renounce privilege because of the justice of history. What type of Christianity would be able to deal with that? He writes:

> Today you will be baptized a Christian. All those great ancient words of the Christian proclamation will be spoken over you and the command of Jesus Christ to baptize will be carried out on you, without your knowing anything about it. But we are once again being driven right back to the beginning of our understanding. Reconciliation and redemption, regeneration and the Holy Spirit, love of our enemies, cross and resurrection, life in Christ and Christian discipleship – all these things are so difficult and so remote that we hardly venture any more to speak of them. In the traditional words and acts we suspect that there may be something quite new and revolutionary, though we cannot as yet grasp or express it.[217]

He continues that Christianity had in some ways become eviscerated of meaning because it had become enslaved to the desire for preservation. And now, its form was changing, hopefully for conversion and purification. Because of the failure of Christianity in the face of the Nazis the old wineskins were shown as of no use and certainly unable to contain the new wine that was ready to pour forth. Bonhoeffer didn't quite know what this was but the question was on his lips, 'What is bothering me incessantly is the question what Christianity really is, or indeed who Christ really is, for us today.'[218]

This as of yet unknown future would be one where the person of faith would once more be able to say a word about God that 'the world will be changed and renewed by it.' This language will not necessarily be in the traditional words or forms he previously mentioned, rather, 'It will be a new language, perhaps quite non-religious, but liberating and redeeming – as was Jesus' language; it will shock people and yet overcome them by its power, it will be the language of a new righteousness and truth, proclaiming God's peace with men and the coming of his kingdom.'[219]

How does faith find a new language from which to speak? How do we find the ability to say something about what Christianity is today that does not run in the same old religious ruts? How can a Christianity so assimilated into the world of modernity convey something of the revolutionary power that is contained in the Gospel witness to Jesus Christ? Perhaps we have said too many words already and we must learn how to speak the new languages by starting in silence. Bonhoeffer knew that this might have to be the genesis of the new language: 'When the Church speaks rightly out of a proper silence, then Christ is proclaimed.'[220] Bonhoeffer himself had been silenced not by God, but by the state, for his very faithfulness to the language of God.[221] He knew some things about silence that most do not have the occasion to know. But this silence cannot slip into complacency about the world in which the language about God must be spoken.

---

[217] *LPP*, pp. 299–300.

[218] Ibid., p. 279.

[219] Ibid., p. 300.

[220] Dietrich Bonhoeffer, *Christ the Center*, trans. John Bowden (New York, NY: Harper and Row, 1966), p. 27.

[221] This was not only the case with the closing of Finkenwalde by the Gestapo, but it also appears in numerous documents of the Nazi regime that exiled Bonhoeffer from Berlin and also forbade him to teach. See, for instance, the exchanges between Bonhoeffer and the Nazi authorities over just such matters in *Conspiracy and Imprisonment*, pp. 180–95.

Silence can serve faith because it creates the space for reflection and discipline so that when a word is spoken it speaks the truth from a place that does not originate with the wisdom of the world order. In fact the willingness to embrace silence, to not speak of every thought, to be patient, means that faith can become the means by which we cultivate the ability to discern what the world really looks like. To pierce the veil of propaganda that the powers throw over those under their sway, to penetrate through the wall of lies and deceit erected by those massive forces Bonhoeffer critiques, is one of the few remaining powers of the Christian in today's world.

Bonhoeffer deeply understood that the world is able to construct itself in such a way that hides the true nature of what is really going on. He addresses this in *Ethics* in a section on 'Ethics as Formation' in which he addresses the failure of everyone, even the ethical theorists, to prepare themselves for the Nazi onslaught. His ability to realize early on the dangers that the National Socialists represented may be found in many aspects of his character, but it was certainly shaped by his faith: 'A person is simple who in the confusion, distortion, and the inversion of all concepts keeps in sight only the single truth of God.'[222]

For Bonhoeffer, it is the person who stands on faith who can pierce through the justifications modernity offers itself and call into question the world that feeds so many into the sacrificial jaws of war and greed. Just for starters, consider the fact that we have seen a military–industrial complex develop in America over the last several decades that creates a gravity that pulls us towards the use of military force. At first the system was able to sustain itself in the 'cold war' era on the basis of building weapons that would ensure that no war was ostensibly necessary. Now, with the new situation we have seen the emergence of private contractors into the securing of the nation–state. One wonders, given the institutions in play, if we have entered a new era where hot wars become necessary to feed the coffers of the new mercenaries and arms merchants. Here the relationship between capitalism and war becomes its most pronounced. Perhaps even more damaging is that we become locked into this rationality to the extent we cannot envision another way of life.

Throughout his life Bonhoeffer offered a different analysis that often ran counter to the prevailing wisdom of the 'world come of age' found in Germany. In his tracing out the tracks laid by the emergence

---

[222] *Ethics*, p. 81.

of technology and its rationality we mentioned earlier, he shows how even the technology itself becomes oddly autonomous, possessing a power all of its own. Technology and the rationality behind it no longer function as an instrument in humankind's control, but it becomes a power with its own inner dynamic: 'The technology of the modern West has freed itself from every kind of service. Its essence is not service but mastery, mastery over nature.'[223]

In Bonhoeffer's discerning gaze, we find echoes of something we have mentioned before, the analysis of historical forces leads one to the conclusion that we have built our own prisons, our own 'iron cages' as Max Weber called them. What is worse is that we have not really stopped to consider what manner of life these structures of state or market have brought us. These forces have been put into play in such a way that the dynamic power of them becomes a force that cannot be hindered or effectively resisted, much less stopped.

The dynamics of modernity have constructed for us the 'iron cage' that has led both to loss of freedom (while yet claiming falsely that we have more freedom than ever), and an almost irreversible loss of meaning (where our identity is reduced to identity by consumption). By loss of freedom I mean we are caught in the world we have constructed in such a way that we are not able to imagine new ways of being in the world through our political or economic structures. This may change in the future as it becomes clear that our very survival depends on new ways of forming our lives, but for now we seem to run along certain tracks that determine for us how we shall live.

Accompanying us in our imprisonment is the soul-destroying spirit that tells us salvation rests in the present orders of either the state or the market. Modernity itself carries its own soteriology, its own theological languages of ultimacy. We are free we are told, but what is not disclosed to us is that our freedom only extends to the boundaries that the state and market allow.

Thus the 'world come of age' has constructed its citizens. Docile and compliant they go on their way hoping their families are fed and their children will have better lives than they did. These in and of themselves are not bad desires, but we become so caught up in the narratives of modernity's salvific strategies we fail to comprehend that others have the same hopes and dreams, but their hopes will be deferred or extinguished because they do not participate in the systems presently in place.

[223] Ibid., p. 116.

What is even more dangerous for us is this system feeds on us in such a way that there are winners and losers. This spawns great anger in those whom it exploits because they can see through the media what they are denied access to. The lifestyle of the haves is always just a little bit out of reach for the have-nots, even though they can see it on the television screen. We are so enmeshed within this order of being we are unable to find new languages to address it. We are at the mercy of those who have the power to shape the story we live within.

Some who sense the utter nihilism of this order seek their refuge in religion, but this is only a temporary salve and offers no real lasting remedy for what ails them. I remember very distinctly on the Sunday after the attacks of 11 September the church that I was attending was standing room only. The size of the congregation swelled as persons sought the solace of God in the face of wanton destruction. In subsequent weeks attendance returned to normal as life went on. This is the type of religion that flees into the projections of our hopes and fears, the type that Bonhoeffer critiqued. Bonhoeffer offers no peace to those who look for God in the space of human weakness.

He did anticipate though that the possibility for something new and revolutionary rests beneath the religious forms and language of the traditions of Christianity. Speaking of it was one way to make it public, but there was also another path that was yet more powerful, and potentially even more subversive to the vast powers that seek to channel and control our lives. This path was found in the community of those who practised the discipline of the secret, or as others have interpreted it, 'arcane discipline'.

We recall that one of Bonhoeffer's central concerns focused on his idea of Christ becoming real in the believing community, but this gave rise to the difficulty of what happens if that community was anything but reflective of Christ. How could the church make known the revolutionary and costly grace that Bonhoeffer embraced? In prison, he seems to be moving back to the community in Finkenwalde by implying that God's self-revelation is concretized most strongly in the community that was able to keep the discipline of the secret.

Historically this idea referred to the fact that the church maintained a discipline over the Eucharist whereby only the baptized could partake, and the path to that baptism itself often took years of instruction. There was a discipline and commitment to faith that served to strengthen it in its conflict with the empire. This was not a faith one could be born into. Though Bonhoeffer did not necessarily have precisely this in mind, he did realize that for the church to be conformed to Christ a different type of discipline was necessary to face the forces that ruled his age.

Perhaps the way to form a community that is effective in its resistance is to not make membership in the state within which one is born equivalent to membership in the body of Christ. In the aftermath of the Reformation the state church became a cultural artefact such that to be born in Denmark, say, meant one was considered a Christian. This made discernment difficult for the Christian because who could stand against all they had been shaped by? The powers that held sway in the world of Bonhoeffer had overcome all resistance to their destructive energies and Christendom was impotent. What good is Jesus when you are so assimilated into your own culture you cannot see any distance between your culture and the Gospel?

He asks questions about this in the letter to Bethge on 30 April 1944 where he probes the whole issue of Christianity's relation to religion and raises the question of religionless Christianity.[224] As we have previously discussed, the paradox in his writing is that the Christian is called out from her religion into a world whereby a new and different order is revealed, and in this world new realities must make themselves known. It is here where the discipline of the secret finds expression:

> In that case Christ is no longer an object of religion, but something quite different, really the Lord of the world. But what does that mean? What is the place of worship and prayer in a religionless situation? Does the secret discipline, or alternatively the difference (which I have suggested to you before) between penultimate and ultimate take on new importance here?[225]

He follows up his thoughts in a letter written on 5 May 1944 in which he takes up the topic of religionlessness again. He treats the themes we have been exploring to state that the question of personal salvation is irrelevant for him. The question of saving one's soul doesn't even appear in Hebrew Scripture, which focuses instead on faithfulness to God in this life as being of primary importance. His interest in these narratives led him to become particularly concerned with the worldly dimensions of faith.

He argues that there are shades of understanding faith that necessitate a type of skill: '. . . that means that a secret discipline must be restored whereby the *mysteries* of the Christian faith are protected

---

[224] *LPP*, p. 280.
[225] Ibid., p. 281.

against profanation.'[226] But, and this is crucial, this type of discipline should not leave the world to its own devices, but translate the language of faith into language that can address the world in all its worldliness, and perhaps even transform it.

As he struggled with the shape that faith assumes in the world of the Nazis, the discipline of the secret was Bonhoeffer's partial answer about how the type of faith to live in the 'world come of age' might secure its boundaries within the world. While immersed within the world in the most profound way, the community of 'arcane discipline' would not drown in the waters of modernity. These boundaries were not to be protected because of a desire for personal piety, or the religious path of withdrawal from the world, rather the mysteries of the church were to be guarded and protected lest they become reduced to something that does not bear the power of God in the world.

Trying to navigate the tensions of attachment and detachment inherent in this paradoxical theology, Bonhoeffer struggled in his thinking to work out the ways in which Christ exists as the community, established among believers. The problem was that the church had taken shape primarily as a religious community, whose belief in God stopped at the door of state hegemony. He clearly understood that Christ exists beyond the boundaries of the church, even within the realm of the so-called profane. It is one of the reasons that he so rejected two spheres thinking.[227] If this were the case, however, what use is a church, or a community of faith?

Does not the cultivation of the discipline of the secret serve as a religious attempt to flee the world into some self-protected space? How does the church maintain the identity to which it is called and not remove itself from all that surrounds it? If it maintains its worldly solidarity with the citizens of modernity does it not risk the eroding of its distinctiveness?

> Finally, how can the experts of the discipline of the secret identify in a spirit infused manner with the citizens of the profane world, when the structures of domination that prevail in the world threaten to subvert the very possibility of a genuine collective solidarity.[228]

---

[226] Ibid., p. 286.

[227] *Ethics*, pp. 57–75. This is just one place in the text that Bonhoeffer addresses this.

[228] Kenneth Surin, 'Comtemptus Mundi and the Disenchanted World: Bonhoeffer's "Discipline of the Secret" and Adorno's "Strategy of Hibernation"' *Journal of the American Academy of Religion*, vol. 53, No. 3 (Sep., 1985), p. 396.

This is the crucial question Bonhoeffer faced and it confronts us today with a special urgency. What, ultimately, shapes our lives, sustains us, offers to nourish us with the hope of something other than what the state and market offer? If we are to be immersed within the world, sharing Christ's own sufferings, what type of citizens are we to be in this moment? Does our language express something revolutionary in the world, or is it the same tired religious platitudes? In the midst of our struggles how do we live out solidarity with the religionless while maintaining faith?

Though the actual phrase 'arcane discipline' only occurs twice in the prison letters, the concerns that rest behind that phrase are deeply rooted in Bonhoeffer's thinking from earlier in his life. This question of how we are shaped was never a peripheral one for Bonhoeffer. Even at Finkenwalde, Bonhoeffer was exploring the early Christian practice of excluding the uninitiated and unbaptized from the second part of the liturgy in which communion was celebrated.[229]

At Tegel he reflected on ways that traditional words and concepts of the church could be expressed that would reveal something other than religious ways of speaking. Could there be in the 'arcane discipline' the key to how a new language could confront the world? For Bonhoeffer it began with prayer and worship. This is a genuine worship and not the watered down worship of communities that worship at the altars of power, or give praise to an all-powerful God who is the guarantor of society's ordering.

It is not found in communities that preach absolute obedience to an order that generates violence and destruction. It is not found in the congregation of souls being shaped to blindness about the ways that God's will is neglected and ignored in the world. This discipline is not found in superficial massaging of person's emotions, or the manifestations of cheap grace that manipulate by guilt.

Bonhoeffer struggled with where such a church could be found and in some measure he believed it was not going to be located in any community that would embrace the privileges of Christianity in its traditional forms. As his musings in the 'Outline for a Book' make clear, Bonhoeffer had rejected all forms of the church that sought its own

---

[229] Bethge, p. 881.

survival at the expense of the oppressed.[230] But how might the practice of the discipline shape the community of Christian faith?

A community that roots its identity in the discipline of the secret is not a church that withdraws into its own self-righteousness, but attunes itself to the world's heartfelt cries and hopelessness. It can view the world without the illusions it is asked to accept by the reigning powers. Its worship will not be made known in the desire to just feel at peace for a minute, because its collective orientation is not to make a person feel good about life as it is. Its theology will not concentrate its attention into explorations of God's abstract powers, without an understanding of how power works in the here and now. And, most assuredly, it will not busy itself with protecting its space against encroachment by the world because it lives in the world in a completely different way that will not allow the world to subvert it with subtle temptations of state endorsement.[231]

'Arcane discipline' will not allow the Gospel to become perverted by those who seek to compromise away Christ's call to be peacemakers in the midst of our self and corporate justifications for more war. It does not count the numbers of its members or mind the dictates of 'church growth' because it is not ultimately concerned with institutional maintenance. It seeks to know and do the will of God in the here and now, not waiting for the by and by.

Still, the suspicion lingers does it not? Is this just another attempt to establish what will at the end be decidedly religious?[232] Concerned with its own purity, how can such a church be anything other than the repository of self-righteous Inquisitors? How does this community exist in such a way that protects it against its own false consciousness? Does this not constitute flight from the world and thus become religious? Does the boundary that the discipline of the secret establishes not become its own iron cage of imprisonment?

This is where Bonhoeffer made clear that the sole reason for this community is to make Jesus Christ known in the world. This is not the

---

[230] *LPP*, p. 381. Of particular interest here is his brief comments in section c of Chapter 1. He wonders where faith in Christ might be found in the traditional forms of the church and appears to consider that Jesus is disappearing from sight.

[231] Ibid. This, of course, was what was at the heart of the tensions in Germany, but this is no less true today. Most radical of all, given the tradition in which he stands is his statement that the church must sell everything it has, the clergy must live on free-will offerings, and 'take the field' on behalf of those caught in the vise of the powers.

[232] As mentioned previously, Luther himself entertained this for a time.

triumphant Jesus of the political order, the Jesus who baptizes the empire in the waters of justification for violence. It is not the Jesus who takes us to a heaven removed from earthly realities. Those who are compelled by faith in Christ to worldly solidarity do not turn away from the world, but towards it: 'In Christ we are invited to participate in the reality of God and the reality of the world at the same time, *the one not without the other.*'[233]

This notion of participation became important for Bonhoeffer and he mentions it several times in the writings from prison as well as the *Ethics.* This participation in the life of God is also a participation in the life of the world:

> Just as the reality of God has entered the reality of the world in Christ, what is Christian cannot be had otherwise than in what is worldly, the 'supernatural' only in the natural, the holy only in the profane, the revelational only in the rational.[234]

The church does not exist to serve itself. It serves the Gospel of Christ, which calls persons from the captivities that bind them to a new life in Christ. This Gospel can be profoundly unsettling.

While Bonhoeffer's conversion does suggest that this new life is personally appropriated, it cannot stay in the realm of the private. Faith finds public expression. Like Abraham's call to leave the homeland, religionless Christianity invites the disciple of the secret to detach from the transitory present order and journey to new truths. Only in this detachment can the disciple find the ability and distance to see the truth and proclaim it.

Those who practise the discipline of the secret become citizens of a new world and can tell the truth to a world that constructs its subjects in such a way that they exist to serve the causes of powers that are ultimately dehumanizing. The citizens of the community of the arcane discipline are freed from the illusions and delusions that previously imprisoned them, because they suffer conversion to a new faith. This faith offers new narratives out of which to live and creates the space to question the assumptions of the 'world come of age'. They can ask why we have built social orders in such a way that a humane and just social and economic order is rendered nearly impossible because the

---

[233] *Ethics*, p. 55. In this section on 'Christ, Reality, and the Good', Bonhoeffer lays out all the reasons why there can be no separation between God and the world that exists in static, metaphysical separation.

[234] Ibid., p. 59.

inevitability of the present world has been rendered as a given, a necessity, which cannot be changed.

The disciples of the secret have been freed by a costly grace in order to tell the truth from the lie. They are able to see that oftentimes what is called 'natural' is but a cloud of unknowing that obscures the fact that we constructed and justified these orders, often in the name of God. Because we have been freed by Christ from obeisance to those orders, we can envision other possibilities of how to live in the world. We are not at the mercy of the hate that distorts human relationship and destroys the possibility of reconciliation. The community formed by the discipline of the secret is able to ask the world why it remains oblivious to the screams of its victims. This community possesses the possibility of not being compromised or subverted by the 'world come of age'. It is a community of subversion that calls all social orders, especially those who use religion to legitimate themselves, into question.

GATHERED AT THE TABLE

This may all seem somewhat idealistic, to believe that the church can reconstitute itself in such a way that it serves as a manifestation of God's reign within earthly life. Where have we ever seen such a thing in the history of the Christian religion? As a way into what I want us to consider we may recall that once Christendom took responsibility in some measure for Caesar's sword it was reduced to providing some measure of legitimation for the empire. This did have profound effects for the future of the church since it meant that changes were inevitable that would change the face of Christianity. Whether one sees this as a positive or negative, the church was enormously affected by this move. The church could influence the kingdom or empire and did so in significant ways, but its identity was affected as well once it entered into the realm of letting the empire dictate to it the way it was to be in the world.

Christianity allowed itself to be pushed into the sphere of the private during the historical processes that followed the Reformation and so as a certain type of rationality gained ascendancy in the West, religion, essentially Christianity, was pushed further to the periphery of the stage, leaving other actors to assume prominence. These are complex narratives and relationships, but the major point I wish to make here is that the relationship between church and state shifted to effect a certain domestication of the church. In countries coming out of the

Reformation, like Germany, the church was accorded a particular type of status by the state, but the boundaries were protected by the state in return for the church's support. Thus by the time we get to the Nazi regime if the church failed to offer unquestioning support, the state moved to destroy it.

Bonhoeffer rejected this attempt by the state to fence in the church, but he saw the result in the church's inability and weakness to resist the state when the time of darkness in the shadow of the National Socialists enveloped his country. Unfortunately, we have seen that a particular expression of Christianity welcomed the National Socialists and was in alignment with them regarding Judaism and the 'Jewish problem'. The Christian church in Germany was the result of centuries of enculturation that led unfortunately to the Nazi regime. Germany, however, is not unique to this dynamic because Christianity in its religious guise, can manifest the same aspects; scapegoating, worship of authoritarianism, and the desire for purity can be found in our day as well.

Bonhoeffer's theology was constantly probing for ways in which Christian identity could be secured from the acids of a religion that delivered itself into the hands of the state. He was not able to find such a church, nor could he create such a church, though it was not for lack of trying. He knew the flaws that existed in such an attempt in renewing the church because it did not have the resources for resistance, though this is not to forget the contributions that many brave souls made.

In his evoking the discipline of the secret we gather a clue as to one avenue of approach to this question. One answer comes in the sacrament that was to be protected, the Eucharist.[235] This can be tricky because the Eucharist in and of itself can become another manifestation of religion, as Bonhoeffer understood it. This act can be an empty one, devoid of any real worship. It may be an act that is done for social propriety, or as a cultural artefact of the religion of Christianity.

---

[235] The Eucharist has been the topic of renewed interest among many theologians and church communities recently. One person who has worked extensively in this area is William T. Cavanaugh. In books such as *Torture and Eucharist: Theology, Politics, and the Body of Christ* (Oxford and Malden, MA: Blackwell Publishers, 1998), and the previously mentioned *Theopolitical Imagination: Discovering the Liturgy as a Political Act in an Age of Consumerism*, he explores the social and political dimensions of the Eucharist and finds in the bread and wine of Christ's supper the means by which the church's body becomes a countervailing sign to the world of a reality that the world does not attend to in these present days.

There is nothing inherent in the Eucharist itself that leads to the formation of persons who renew and transform the world. Yet for those who enter into the *mystery* of the meal, lives are transformed.

Arcane discipline is concerned primarily with the shape the church assumes in the world, the commitments it makes, the way it shapes and forms persons for discipleship. It is ultimately about identity and even though the boundary of a different type of Christian faith can never be totally protected from the influence of an acculturated religion, there are certain habits the religionless Christian can cultivate, certain disciplines to embrace, that do shape identity towards something new and different in the world.

It is in the Eucharist that we find the potential means whereby the church starts its growth into its identity as the concrete expression of Christ on earth. Partly this is because the Eucharist structures time and space for us in such a way that we are re-membered into a worldly body that transcends the boundaries that the 'world come of age' has constructed for us. Its liturgy narrates the reality of Christ's life, death and resurrection that constitutes the basis for our commitments in life.

This new body, nourished in the bread and wine, transgresses those boundaries that the political order wishes to impose in order to maintain its dominance. This body potentially exists in the fullest sense of the word as an ecumenical body. This ecumenicity though is not a foregone conclusion, and even today does not make an appearance in concrete reality everywhere. The division of the churches shows this to be the tragic case. However, in the discipline of the secret, worship, engaged in with the desire to have communion with God and one another, creates the possibilities for the formation of a radical and global community. Our primary allegiance is to be the body of Christ in the world, in whatever form we can. But, it most definitely comes to visible life in the sacrament of the table.

This ecumenicity of the body of Christ made visible in the bread and wine subverts the state's pretensions to our ultimate allegiance and stands as a judgement on a world that seeks to divide persons. Politics as presently practised in the power centres of the world is the art of dividing people from one another, and the table where persons of faith gather stands in contradistinction to these divisions. Engaged in as discipline and practice, and not religious/cultural ritual, the Eucharist shapes us to understand the world in different ways than the prevailing ethos does.

This is one of the reasons that the Nazis were so adamantly opposed to Bonhoeffer's involvement in the ecumenical movement. They rightly understood that Christians who saw themselves bound and connected to a Lord who transcends the temporal bonds of nation or family would not serve the cause of their quest for dominance. The state and its orders are not the primary agents for identity formation for those formed around the table of the risen Christ.

In fact, inasmuch as the state's natural order appears to be violence, any gathering around a table where a genuine and non-coerced peace reigns constitutes a threat to those who want to manipulate populations to take up arms against those who threaten the regime. This violence has generated conditions that have created the alienation and violence, the estrangement and terror we are presently plagued with. How these habits are ever overcome perplexes so many that we simply give up in the face of such overwhelming forces. But, if Bonhoeffer's perceptions carry weight today, then the necessary discipline for a new order starts with prayer, worship and the Eucharist as a vital part of that. Even here, though, something new must make itself known.

The gathering around the table of the gift means a reorientation to life is in order. The relationships we establish and nourish in the world are reconfigured to the creation of a different type of person in the world. Our vision is expanded by participation in this meal to include all those not present:

> In the Eucharist, we receive the gift of Christ not as mere passive recipients, but by being incorporated into the gift itself, the Body of Christ. As members of the Body, we then become nourished by others – including those not part of the visible Body – in the unending trinitarian economy of gratuitous giving and joyful reception.[236]

In this meal the boundaries we erect, the territories we mark, the identities we construct on foundations other than the desire for God's life to be made present in this existence, are potentially erased in favour of a different formation, a different community. In this community Christ exists at the centre of the table and among the peripheries, present in those on the margins, even those not present at the table. Participation in this meal means that I enter into the life of God because in this meal a space opens up for new languages and practices.

This communion stands as a threat to all other calls for unity based on nation, family, ethnicity or political affiliation. Rather, the communion of the table opens the possibility that our imaginations can actually entertain fighting for reconciliation to replace enmity, and

---

[236] *Theopolitical Imagination*, pp. 48–49.

forgiveness of sins to become a way of life, for redemption to have its say. In this way, when I leave the table and seek those goods of God in creation I do not have my own self-interests at heart. Turning my face to the Other I do not wish their destruction, for God has encountered me through them.

Though Bonhoeffer was not able to flesh this out because of his untimely death, he saw clearly that how the Body of Christ forms itself has consequences for the rest of the world. In the address at Fanø Bonhoeffer argued that the church must transgress boundaries that were national, political, social and racial. Persons gathered around the Eucharistic table were bound to one another by Christ far more intently than by common history, blood, class or language. Though these ties of land, nation and ethnicity are important, they are ultimately penultimate in the presence of Christ. His commandment of peace is more powerful and binding than historically contingent identities. They take up arms against Christ if they take up arms against one another because the church of Christ lives at one and the same time in everyone among all nations.[237]

In his 'Outline for a Book' Bonhoeffer wrote that faith is participation in the being of Jesus, incarnation, cross and resurrection. This relation to God is not to the highest and greatest thing we can imagine, rather it is a relation that re-orders our relations to others: '. . . our relation to God is a new life in "existence for others", through participation in the being of Jesus. The transcendental is not infinite and unattainable tasks, but the neighbour who is within reach in any given situation.'"[238]

We participate in this being of Jesus by the gift that binds us to the risen Lord. This participation is a new life in the existence for others. He was concerned in this outline about what we believe enough to stake our very lives on. He sensed that the church was going to have to recreate its being in the world and this cannot be a parochial church because the church that is formed by ties other than those mediated by the grace of Eucharist won't be strong enough to stand in the days of darkness.

Participation in Christ is participation in this meal of bread and wine which proclaims at its heart God's reconciliation with the world through Christ. For the religionless Christian this means not just the

[237] *NRS*, p. 290.
[238] *LPP*, p. 381.

foretaste of some otherworldly, heavenly unity, but the practice of peace and reconciliation within the earthly community. In this way, the Eucharist can transfigure the boundaries established by the state and all other orders that ask for our allegiance, or work covertly to convert us to their logics and worldviews.

The Eucharist transforms speech and imagination by its act and speech and establishes the grounds within which we can be re-membered and nourished into the larger community of faith, beyond the limitations imposed on us by regimes of violence. The eucharistic community exists in order to bear witness to different visions to a world in love with its own destruction. The discipline of the secret is not constructed on the basis of coercion, though violence is present in the body and blood of Christ.

This violence of the cross stands in judgement upon all orders of state or religion, which in their fear crucify those whose only crime is that they present an alternative to the world's arrangements. The arcane discipline of the Eucharist, graced with the presence of Christ, provides a space within which the church stands as a witness that the community of peace is possible if we will only have the courage, discernment and wisdom to fight for it. The risks of being nourished by this table and participating in this supper are enormous.

These risks will be made evident pretty quickly once the church confronts the state's hegemonic power to construct our world. The church of the Eucharist cannot be absorbed by the alien principalities and powers which seek to structure the very identities of its citizens. It does not vacate the space by which the world interprets itself by withdrawal into the private sphere that religion, as it has been framed by modernity, claims as the only acceptable space of existence.

To those who have not been formed by these graces this sounds like pretty thin grounds to stand resistant to the powers that presently dominate the world, but this is only to suggest that Christians have not really understood or embraced the implications of a faith that lives out of a different commitment than to the society we live within. In the Eucharist, we find the potential to be formed in such a way as to resist all orders that arrange the world to pursue goods that are not God's desire for the creation. The question of how effective this resistance becomes in the face of so much that opposes it is not really the right question to ask, rather what opens to us when faithfulness to this table guides our lives becomes the issue.

So, we return to the major questions Bonhoeffer asks – Who Is Jesus Christ? What is Christianity for us today? And along with these core questions is Bonhoeffer's further question of: 'What do we really believe? I mean, believe in such a way that we stake our very lives on it?'[239] Is there a place, concretely, where we can point to that would allow us to see the practice of arcane discipline?

On the wall of martyrs at Westminster there is another figure who also lost his life in conflict with the political orders of the day, Oscar Romero. Romero was the Archbishop of El Salvador during a time of civil war that damaged that country with much violence. Several years ago there was a movie made about Romero's life. One of the things that has always struck me about that movie is the way that the script-writers used moments of Romero's life to tell his story. One of the striking aspects of this narrative structure was the way the celebration of the Eucharist was framed in such a way that it provided the means of resistance to the forces of oppression.

Of course, this was because the Eucharist stood at the centre of Romero's community and so functioned as the focus of the church. In much of the movie the Eucharist stood at the heart of the conflict with militaristic oppression. In most scenes except the first and last the military backed down when the celebration of the Eucharist began. At the end, when Romero is celebrating Eucharist and is assassinated within the cathedral by a lone gunman, we see a profound truth. What the military could not do in public because the community's voice in Eucharist was an effective force against it, had to be done in private. Some would argue that this just shows how ineffective Christian witness is in the world today. Do we not understand how serious the situation is? Romero was exemplary, but in the end he was assassinated. How can that help?

This is why the entire ecumenical community is so vitally important, because the powers we face are too strong to resist as individuals. The liturgy of authentic worship in word and table narrates, creates, sustains and nourishes a community that can be radically destabilizing. This community is composed of many members, from different nations, who gather around many tables, all containing the bread and wine which binds us, to celebrate forgiveness of sins and reconciliation of the estranged. The more visible this community becomes, the more present it becomes in the world. Those forces that seek to dominate the world through coercive powers can only defeat the life this community brings by dis-membering us from one another.

---

[239] *LPP*, p. 382.

In the community's embrace of a reality that transcends all contingent arrangements, we find a power being made known in powerlessness. The embrace of the powerlessness of God becomes the ultimate subversion of a world that seeks to build on violence and coercive power. The powerlessness of God that Bonhoeffer ponders in Tegel is not the instantiation of his own weakness, rather it is the deep spiritual awareness that powerlessness does not entail weakness in the face of oppression and violence. It means the resources exist for a power that the powers do not have the means to access, for this comes only from those willing to lay down arms and gather at the table to be reconciled to God and one another.

The 'world come of age' seeks to domesticate Christian witness into the channels of privatized religion or the comforts of civil religion. This is true not just with Christian faith, but any faith commitment that makes claims on the public square. It seeks our allegiance to its idols of the state and market, and in deifying some abstract notion of the individual it denies the worldly and international commonality of the table. But, those who are prepared to enter into the discipline of the secret and all that stands behind it become empowered to offer something different to the world. The willingness of the church to suffer with the world offers the possibility that the church can tell truths the 'world come of age' cannot hear in its self-imposed captivity. It may well be the case that even modernity's citizens know there are truths to be told:

> Once it has recognized the ruling universal order and its proportions as sick – and marked in the most literal sense with paranoia, with 'pathic projection' – then it can see as healing cells only what appears, by the standards of that order as itself sick, eccentric, paranoia – indeed, 'mad'; and it is true today as in the Middle Ages that only fools tell their masters the truth.[240]

A TALE OF TWO TRADITIONS

We come to a significant paradox contained in Bonhoeffer. All the traditions that deliver the church to the position of ineffectual weakness must suffer conversion. Christianity must become in some way free of its religious impulses. The church had emerged in such a way because

---

[240] Theodore Adorno, *Minima Moralia*, trans. by E. F. N. Jephcott (London: Verso, 1974), 73. Quoted from Surin, 401.

the path it took led it to acquiescence to the Nazis. This path resulted from a 'heavy incubus of difficult traditional ideas.'[241] Does this mean that religionless Christianity must take leave of tradition at the end of the day? Has the church of Constantine led to such captivity that we are left bereft of resources to resist the life being pushed on us?

In this search for a new language Bonhoeffer did not mean that the ideas of repentance, reconciliation, salvation, as such were to be totally jettisoned. They must be recovered in such a way that the truths to which they attest can be heard without all the trappings of tradition that had domesticated them in the first place. The words and ideas may need to be deconstructed in order that the power behind them might become living realities in the world. If recovery of the worldly dimensions of the Eucharist leads Christianity to see with fresh eyes and heart the revolutionary power and grace that rests at its centre, what would it look like if similar recovery could be made of other traditions in Christianity? Religionlessness does not mean a lack of faith, it points to the incognito that lies underneath the present forms.

Christopher Morse in his fascinating systematic theology, *Not Every Spirit: A Dogmatics of Christian Unbelief*, makes the point that appeal to tradition can be somewhat slippery. This is because the word 'tradition' can function as a verb or a noun. In the Christian Scripture, the meaning of the word 'traditioning' is that of delivering or handing over something. It conveys the passing along of something important. Morse cites examples in the biblical text which use the word to cite the passing on of the Gospel, conveyed in the word and power that is Jesus Christ by whom humanity is set free and saved. Morse contends that what we see here may be called the tradition of freedom.

There is another meaning to the term, however. In the Passion narratives the betrayal of Jesus is said to have been accomplished by Judas, who 'traditioned' Jesus into the hands of sinners, and Pontius Pilate 'traditioned' Jesus to crucifixion. Those who criticize the disciples for breaking the tradition are rebuked by Jesus in Matthew 15:6: 'So, for the sake of your traditions you make void the word of God.'

These two meanings of the word tradition emerge from the narratives to offer different perspectives. One leads to the Christ who sets us free from that which would oppress us, the other meaning leads us to the Christ who stands as a symbol of our religious projections.

---

[241] *LPP*, p. 381.

The story of Christianity can be seen as a conflict between these traditions: the tradition of freedom and the tradition of betrayal. Both of these trajectories are ancient and have continued throughout the history of Christianity.[242]

The tensions between these competing traditions can be found throughout the life of the church as there has always been a desire to legitimate the status quo of political and ecclesial power with the imprimatur of the divine. It is this tradition that allowed the German Christians to claim that they stood on the basis of a historic and 'positive' Christianity. This is the tradition of the religious, the tradition that legitimates whatever is as the will of God.

But the voice of the German Christians was not the only tradition expressed. The other stream, the tradition of freedom, has found expression in those who have resisted throughout history. One of the most distinctive marks of the countercultural tradition is the way in which it uses Scripture to retrieve a way of understanding Jesus Christ. In Bonhoeffer's mind the incarnation of God in Christ is such that any parochial or political baptism of this Christ to further an agenda rooted in violence, oppression, or national and ethnic identity negates the reality of God. The identity of Jesus Christ as truly God and truly human means that any confession of a power manifest in human history that brings evil masquerading as good, or oppression cloaked in the clothes of faith, or obedience to national duty that calls for the death of others, must be regarded with suspicion.

The freedom given us by faith in Jesus Christ means that we are freed from all those prisons that the prevailing orders use to construct our identities and hearts. We are freed to call the world's goods evil when they result in oppression and injustice, even when the evil occurs in the name of justice and peace. It is the freedom of those who know they have been forgiven much and thus can extend reconciliation to a world at enmity. This freedom breaks the cycles of hatred and violence that fuel and torment the world today. It possesses the ability to see the sinfulness present in all sides of conflict and offer a different path to those who repent.

---

[242] Christopher Morse, *Not Every Spirit: A Dogmatics of Christian Unbelief*, (Valley Forge, PA.: Trinity Press International, 1994), pp. 47–48. I have used this illustration previously in *The Matrix of Faith: Reclaiming a Christian Vision*, (New York: Crossroad Publishing Company, 2001).

The religionless Christian is not tied to the spaces that the world seeks to keep her captive to, but becomes at the table of the supper truly catholic, shaped and formed by participation in the life, teachings, death and resurrection of Christ. In freedom we accept the reality that we are not innocent and are responsible for the world, but in this solidarity with the sin of the world we are not engulfed by the forces that drive it, nor do we have to participate in those sins.[243]

The 'world come of age' needs a Christianity come of age, a Christianity that can ask the right questions and stand together as a global community so that its individuals do not have to feel the burden of sin and guilt for their nations as Bonhoeffer did. These are the concerns that seek a different level of discernment concerning the life of God in the world.

Ultimately, Bonhoeffer's writings reflect the unerring pursuit of someone who is attempting to grasp a truly Christological understanding of God and the world. It is not doctrine that concerns Bonhoeffer as much as it is how life itself is to be lived. What shape does the life of God take in concrete reality? Because the reality was always changing Bonhoeffer never offered absolute and timeless ethics or actions, rather the real situations he found himself in profoundly directed his actions. And sometimes those actions were confused and caused Bonhoeffer great pain and suffering.

For Bonhoeffer there was only one order of Being for the Christian and that was the life that God establishes through God's self-revelation in Christ. At issue in Bonhoeffer's life was how that one reality was to be made known in life itself.[244] In his searching faith Bonhoeffer put before the world a better way of being the world. This does not mean that the church plays by Caesar's rules. Because it has the potential to offer the world a vision that relativizes all social orders, Christianity may perhaps best be shaped in the contemporary setting by commitments that place it in a position of exile.

Bonhoeffer experienced a degree of exile that led to much suffering. But the instincts that led him there are ones that should be cultivated by the church today for the radical tradition of faithfulness to

---

[243] Bonhoeffer's thoughts about how we oppose evil found in *Discipleship* are profoundly compelling in this regard. Many take his neglect of these ideas as evidence of the fact that when we confront evil we must be willing to get our hands dirty. If Bonhoeffer had existed within a community of faithful practice, however, those very same strategies may have been the church's path to resistance.

[244] See, for instance, his treatment of this in *Ethics*, pp. 49–50.

the gospel. Bonhoeffer knew that Christianity would not survive as a living faith if it did not itself suffer conversion. It may survive as a religion, but to find expression as a faith that calls the principalities and powers into question and places the demands of discipleship to God at the centre of life, the religion itself may have to die. Bonhoeffer stands in the stream of the counter-tradition because he did resist. He resisted in ways that we do not and because those who resist are historically so few, the church continues to have little of use to say in the world. This resistance to the orders that presently drive the world is not done in the spirit of self-righteousness, or the desire for power, but in order that the world itself might hear the cry of those who suffer, and respond with a new imagination to the challenges before us.

We do, indeed, live in troubled times, and, though every age is unique in its own way, our time carries distinct challenges. The issue of resources and the environment, the manifestation of increasingly authoritarian regimes to deal with scarcity and social upheaval, the realignment of economic structures, the negotiation of religious difference; these are only a hint at what rests in our future. Bonhoeffer is our companion on this journey and the questions he asks should never leave us, though they might be framed in a different way. We live in a world that arranges itself as if there were no God, and, paradoxically, one where God is employed by humankind to embody our fears and frustrations, as well as our hopes and dreams. What Bonhoeffer struggled with is how God is known in the world. Faith in Christ does not mean primary allegiance to an institution, a religion, or a particular political order. Religionless Christianity, continually on pilgrimage, places us in the midst of a world in love with its own destruction in order that we might manifest God's reconciling and healing presence.

BIBLIOGRAPHY

Barber, Benjamin. *Jihad vs. McWorld*. New York: Ballantine Books, 1996.

Barnett, Victoria. *For the Soul of the People: Protestant Protest against Hitler.* New York: Oxford University Press, 1992.

Barth, Karl. *Church Dogmatics*. Edinburgh, UK: T & T Clark, 1958.

Bauman, Zygmunt. *Modernity and the Holocaust*. Ithaca, NY: Cornell University Press, 1989.

Baynes, Norman H. (ed.). *The Speeches of Adolf Hitler, 1922–1939*, vol. 1. London: Oxford University Press, 1942.

Berger, Peter. *Pyramids of Sacrifice: Political Ethics and Social Change.* Garden City, NY: Anchor, 1976.

___. *The Sacred Canopy: Elements of a Sociological Theory of Religion.* Garden City, NY: Anchor, 1990.

Bethge, Eberhard. *Dietrich Bonhoeffer. A Biography.* Translation revised by Victoria Barnett. Minneapolis, MN: Fortress Press, 2000.

___. *Friendship and Resistance: Essays on Dietrich Bonhoeffer.* Grand Rapids, MI: Eerdmans, 1995.

Bonhoeffer, Dietrich. *Dietrich Bonhoeffer Werke*. 17 vols. ed. Eberhard Bethge, Ernst Feil, Christian Gremmels, Wolfgang Huber, Hans Pfiefer, Albrecht Schönherr and Heinz Eduard Tödt. Munich: Christian Kaiser Verlag, 1986–1999.

___. *Dietrich Bonhoeffer Works* English Edition, ed. Wayne Whitson Floyd Jr, et al. Minneapolis, MN: Augsburg Fortress, 1998–present.

___. *Christ the Center.* Trans. John Bowden. New York: Harper and Row, 1966.

___. *Fiction From Prison.* ed. Renate and Eberhard Bethge with Clifford Green. Philadelphia, PA: Fortress Press, 1981.

___. *Gesammelte Schriften.* ed. Eberhard Bethge. 6 vols. Munich: Christian Kaiser Verlag, 1965–1974.

___. *Letters and Papers from Prison.* The Enlarged Edition. ed. Eberhard Bethge. New York: Macmillan, 1971.

___. *Love Letters from Cell 92: The Correspondence between Dietrich Bonhoeffer and Maria von Wedemeyer, 1943–45.* ed. Ruth-Alice von Bismarck and Ulrich Kabitz. Postscript by Eberhard Bethge. Nashville, TN: Abingdon, 1994.

___. *No Rusty Swords. Letters, Lectures and Notes, 1928–1936, from the Collected Works of Dietrich Bonhoeffer.* vol. 1. ed. Edwin H. Robertson. New York: Harper and Row, 1965.

___. *Preface to Bonhoeffer: The Man and Two of His Shorter Writings.* ed. John D. Godsey. Philadelphia, PA: Fortress Press, 1965.

___. *A Testament to Freedom: The Essential Writings of Dietrich Bonhoeffer.* ed. Geffrey B. Kelly and F. Burton Nelson. San Francisco, CA: Harper, 1995.

Cavanaugh, William. 'A Fire Strong Enough to Consume the House: The Wars of Religion and the Rise of the State,' *Modern Theology.* 11:4. October 1995, pp. 397–420.

___. *Theopolitical Imagination: Discovering the Liturgy as a Political Act in an Age of Global Consumerism.* London and New York: T & T Clark, 2001.

___. *Torture and Eucharist: Theology, Politics, and the Body of Christ,* Challenges in Contemporary Theology, series. New York: Wiley-Blackwell, 1998.

Chandler, Andrew (ed.). *The Terrible Alternative: Christian Martyrdom in the Twentieth Century.* London: Cassell, 2003.

Cochrane, Arthur C. *The Church's Confession Under Hitler.* Philadelphia, PA: Westminster Press, 1962.

de Gruchy, John W. (ed.). *Bonhoeffer for a New Day: Theology in a Time of Transition.* Grand Rapids, MI: Eerdmans, 1997.

___. (ed.). *Cambridge Companion to Dietrich Bonhoeffer.* The Cambridge Companions to Religion Series. Cambridge, UK.: Cambridge University Press, 1999.

___. *Daring, Trusting Spirit: Bonhoeffer's Friend Eberhard Bethge.* Minneapolis, MN: Fortress Press, 2005.

Dostoyevsky, Fyodor. *The Brothers Karamozov.* Trans. David McDuff. New York: Penguin, 1993.

Ericksen, Robert P. and Heschel Susannah (ed.). *Betrayal: German Churches and the Holocaust.* Minneapolis, MN: Fortress Press, 1999.

___. *Theologians under Hitler: Gerhard Kittel, Paul Althaus, and Emmanuel Hirsch.* New Haven, CT: Yale University Press, 1985.

Feil, Ernst. *The Theology of Dietrich Bonhoeffer.* Trans. Martin Rumscheidt. Philadelphia, PA: Fortress, 1985.

Fitzgerald, Timothy. *The Ideology of Religious Studies.* New York and Oxford: Oxford University Press, 2000.

Freud, Sigmund. *The Future of an Illusion.* Trans. and ed. James Strachey New York: W. W. Norton, 1961.

Gay, Graig M. *The Way of the Modern World or, Why it is Tempting to Live as if God Doesn't Exist.* Grand Rapids, MI: Eerdmans, 1998.

Gergen, Kenneth J. *The Saturated Self: Dilemmas of Identity in Contemporary Life.* New York: Basic Books, 1991.

Green, Clifford J. *Bonhoeffer: A Thelogy of Sociality,* rev. ed. Grand Rapids, MI: Eerdmans, 1999.

Hauerwas, Stanley. *Performing the Faith: Bonhoeffer and the Practice of Nonviolence.* Grand Rapids, MI: Brazos Press, 2004.

Haynes, Stephen. *The Bonhoeffer Phenomenon: Portraits of a Protestant Saint.* Minneapolis, MN: Augsburg Fortress, 2004.

—. *The Bonhoeffer Legacy: Post-Holocaust Perspectives* Minneapolis, MN: Augsburg Fortress, 2006.

Hopper, David H. *A Dissent on Bonhoeffer.* Philadelphia, PA: Westminster Press, 1975.

Huntemann, Georg. *The Other Bonhoeffer: An Evangelical Reassessment of Dietrich Bonhoeffer.* Trans. Todd Huizinga. Grand Rapids, MI: Baker, 1993.

Jurgensmeyer, Mark. *Terror in the Mind of God: The Global Rise of Religious Violence.* Berkeley, CA: University of California Press, 2000.

Kelly, Geffrey B. and F. Burton Nelson. *The Cost of Moral Leadership: The Spirituality of Dietrich Bonhoeffer.* Grand Rapids, MI: Eerdmans, 2003.

Long, D. Stephen. *Divine Economy: Theology and the Market.* Radical Orthodoxy Series. London and New York: Routledge, 2000.

___. *The Goodness of God: Theology, Church, and the Social Order.* Grand Rapids, MI: Brazos Press, 2001.

Luther, Martin. *On Temporal Authority: To What Extent it Should be Obeyed.*

Matheson, Peter (ed.). *The Third Reich and the Christian Churches.* Grand Rapids, MI: Eerdmans, 1981.

Mayer, Jane. 'The Black Sites' *The New Yorker Magazine.* 13 August 2007.

Milwaukee Journal Sentinel, 14 May 2004. 'President Bush's Concordia Commencement Speech.' Available at www.jsonline.com/news/oswash/may04/229423.asp, accessed 14 July 2008.

Morse, Christopher. *Not Every Spirit: A Dogmatics of Christian Unbelief.* Valley Forge, PA.: Trinity Press International, 1994.

Peters, Rebecca Todd. *In Search of the Good Life: An Ethics of Globalization.* New York: Continuum, 2006.

Pugh, Jeffrey C. *The Matrix of Faith: Reclaiming a Christian Vision.* New York: Crossroad, 2001.

Rasmussen, Larry L. *Dietrich Bonhoeffer: Reality and Resistance.* Studies in Christian Ethics. Nashville, TN: Abingdon. 1972

___. *Dietrich Bonhoeffer – His Significance for North Americans.* Minneapolis, MN: Fortress Press, 1990.

Roth, Martin. 'Just War, Christians and Iraq – Where is the Justice in Not Attacking?' 29 October 2002, available at www.martinrothonline.com/MRCC36.htm, accessed 14 July 2008.

Schleiermacher, F. D. E. *Speeches on Religion.* Trans. Richard Crouter. Cambridge: Cambridge University Press, 1992.

Slane, Craig J. *Bonhoeffer as Martyr: Social Responsibility and Modern Christian Commitment.* Grand Rapids, MI: Brazos, 2003.

Smith, Robert O. 'Bonhoeffer, Bloggers, and Bush: Uses of a "Protestant Saint" in the Fog of War.' Unpublished paper.

Smith, Wilfred Cantwell. *The Meaning and End of Religion.* New York: Macmillan, 1962.

Soelle, Dorothee. *The Silent Cry: Mysticism and Resistance.* Trans. Barbara and Martin Rumscheidt. Minneapolis, MN: Fortress Press, 2001.

Surin, Kenneth. 'Contemptus Mundi and the Disenchanted World: Dietrich Bonhoeffer's "Discipline of the Secret" and Adorno's "Strategy of Hibernation"'. *Journal of the American Academy of Religion.* vol. 53, No. 3. 1985, pp. 383–410.

Suskind, Ron. 'Without a Doubt' *New York Times Magazine.* 17 October 2004.

Taylor, Charles. *A Secular Age.* Cambridge, MA: Belknap Press, 2007.

___. *The Sources of the Self: The Making of the Modern Identity.* Cambridge, MA: Harvard University Press, 1992.

Tödt, Heinz Eduard. *Authentic Faith: Bonhoeffer's Theological Ethics in Context.* ed. Ernst-Albert Scharffenorth and Glen Harold Stassen. Trans. David Stassen and Ilse Tödt. Grand Rapids, MI: Eerdmans, 2007.

Toulmin, Stephan. *Cosmopolis: The Hidden Agenda of Modernity.* New York: Free Press, 1990.

Volf, Miroslav. *Exclusion and Embrace: A Theological Exploration of I dentity, Otherness, and Reconciliation.* Nashville, TN: Abingdon Press, 1996.

Wüstenberg, Ralf K. *A Theology of Life: Dietrich Bonhoeffer's Religionless Christianity.* Trans. by Doug Stott. Grand Rapids, MI: Eerdmans, 1998.

Žižek, Slavoj. *On Belief.* Thinking in Action Series. London and New York: Routledge, 2001.

___. *The Fragile Absolute or, Why Is the Christian Legacy Worth Fighting for?* London and New York: Verso, 2000.

INDEX